Developing
Research
Questions

A Guide for Social Scientists

PATRICK WHITE

palgrave
macmillan

First published 2009 by
PALGRAVE MACMILLAN

Palgrave Macmillan in the UK is an imprint of Macmillan Publishers Limited, registered in England, company number 785998, of Houndmills, Basingstoke, Hampshire RG21 6XS.

Palgrave Macmillan in the US is a division of St Martin's Press LLC, 175 Fifth Avenue, New York, NY 10010.

Palgrave Macmillan is the global academic imprint of the above companies and has companies and representatives throughout the world.

Palgrave® and Macmillan® are registered trademarks in the United States, the United Kingdom, Europe and other countries.

ISBN-13: 978-1-4039-9815-6
ISBN-10: 1-4039-9815-9

This book is printed on paper suitable for recycling and made from fully managed and sustained forest sources. Logging, pulping and manufacturing processes are expected to conform to the environmental regulations of the country of origin.

A catalogue record for this book is available from the British Library.

Library of Congress Cataloging-in-Publication Data

White, Patrick, 1971–
    Developing research questions : a guide for social scientists /
Patrick White.
        p. cm.
    Includes index.
    ISBN 978–1–4039–9815–6 (alk. paper)
        1. Social sciences – Research – Methodology. I. Title.

H62.W453 2009
300.72—dc22   2008039128

10 9 8 7 6 5 4 3 2 1
18 17 16 15 14 13 12 11 10 09

Printed and bound in China

For BG

Contents

Acknowledgements   ix

Introduction   1
Why should you read a book on research questions?   1
Who is this book for?   2
How should I use this book?   2
The structure of the book   3

1. Where do research ideas come from?   5
Curiosity and surprise: the basis of inquiry   5
The role of the literature: knowing the field   7
The role of theory   22
'Practical' stimuli for research questions   27
Summary   31
Further reading   32

2. What makes a research question?   33
Research topics, aims and objectives   33
The form of questions and their content   35
Question types   47
Hypotheses   53
Summary   58
Further reading   58

3. What makes a question 'researchable'?   59
The 'researchability' of questions   59
A question of language   66
A question of resources   78
Summary   86
Further reading   88

4. Questions, methods and indicators   89
Questions as the starting point of research   89
The importance of research design   97

Operationalizing concepts 99
Summary 110
Further reading 111

5. **Answering research questions:**
   claims, evidence and warrant 112
   The structure of arguments 113
   Claims 114
   Data and evidence 116
   Warrant 117
   Alternative hypotheses 121
   Summary 122
   Further reading 122

Afterword 123

Bibliography 124

Index 131

Acknowledgements

I originally had the idea for this book while working on the *Economic and Social Research Council's* Research Capacity Building Network (RCBN). I would like to thank Chris Taylor and Stephen Gorard for their help and advice and the very useful discussions we had on the subject during the course of that project. I am also very grateful to Martyn Hammersley, Anne Edwards and Peter Kutnick for their contributions to the RCBN Research Questions Workshop that I was responsible for organizing.

I would like to thank Edumund Chattoe-Brown, David Bartram and Alan Bryman, all of who offered me valuable advice, and to Derek Layder, who very generously read and commented on an early copy of the manuscript. I am indebted to both of the anonymous reviewers, who provided me with feedback that was both comprehensive and extremely useful. I would like to express my gratitude to Catherine Gray and Emily Salz, for their initial enthusiasm and support, and to Anna Reeve for managing and co-ordinating the project so diligently.

Finally, I would like to thank Emma Smith, not only for her close reading of many drafts of this book, but for her never-ending patience and support.

Introduction

WHY SHOULD YOU READ A BOOK ON RESEARCH QUESTIONS?

If you are a student studying one of the social sciences – subjects such as sociology, criminology, politics, economics, education and health sciences – it is likely that at some point in your studies you will be required to conduct a research project. The scale and focus of this research will vary depending on your level of study, the subject you are studying and the requirements of the course you are taking, but the essence of the activity will remain the same: trying to find answers to particular questions.

The questions that you pose will be central to your research project. They will dictate the kind of data you need and, in turn, the methods of data collection and analysis that are most appropriate. Different types of questions will require different kinds of answers, and some types of questions are much more challenging to answer than others.

You should not underestimate how difficult or time consuming it can be to develop research questions. Students often find this to be one of the most challenging stages of the research process. Generating ideas for research requires considerable imagination and turning those ideas into clearly formulated questions involves disciplined and logical thought. But time spent thinking about your research questions will pay dividends at later stages of the research.

Before you start designing your research or collecting and analysing any data, it is absolutely vital that you are clear about what you are trying to find out. Many methods textbooks emphasize this point but, unfortunately, few provide much concrete advice in this area. And while there are many specialist texts devoted to exploring other aspects of the research process in considerable detail, there are very few books devoted to the subject of research questions. This book aims to fill that gap and provide useful and practical advice for students and those new to social research.

WHO IS THIS BOOK FOR?

This book is primarily aimed at students and researchers who are conducting small-scale research projects. It caters to a wide audience, from undergraduates, through postgraduates and practitioners, to professional researchers and teachers. It is intended to be sufficiently accessible to be comfortable reading for undergraduate students whilst addressing issues that postgraduates and new career researchers may still find challenging.

Although it focuses primarily on social science research, it provides advice that those in other fields of inquiry such as the humanities, psychology, management and business may also find useful. In fact, anyone conducting an empirical research project will almost certainly find something of use or interest in the following pages. This text can also be used as a resource by those involved in supervising or managing novice researchers.

Because it relates research questions to other aspects of the research process, this book may also be useful to undergraduate and postgraduate students taking research methods courses. However, whilst the early stages of the research process are explored at various points in this book, it is important to point out that research design and the collection and analysis of data are *not* covered in any detail. There are already a large number of texts covering these areas and this book is not intended to replace them. Rather it is intended to *complement* them by providing advice and guidance on a topic that is rarely covered in detail in such texts.

HOW SHOULD I USE THIS BOOK?

How this book is used most profitably will depend on the individual needs of the reader. The chapters are intended to be read in order but readers are invited to skip sections they feel are irrelevant to their specific needs. As some readers may wish to 'dip-in' to particular chapters or sections, each part is written with this in mind and cross-references are included to other relevant discussions.

THE STRUCTURE OF THE BOOK

The first chapter of the book examines the role of research questions in the process of social research. The importance of being genuinely curious about the social world and being prepared to be surprised by what you find out are discussed alongside the consequences of failing to adopt such attitudes. It explores the relationship between new questions and existing knowledge and examines the role of various types of literature in generating and developing research questions. The ways in which ideas for research can be influenced by theory, previous research and policy documents are discussed, and advice on how best to use the various forms of literature is provided. The chapter ends by questioning the extent to which research questions *can* or *should* be 'original' and the degree to which they should be influenced by the work of others.

Chapter 2 highlights particular problems that can arise with the form or content of research questions. It identifies mistakes that are commonly made when formulating research questions and provides advice on how these can be avoided. The advantages gained by moving beyond topics and problems to research questions are explained and the special place of hypotheses in scientific investigation is also discussed. The various ways that different writers have categorized research questions is reviewed and the implications of posing different kinds of question are explored, alongside recommendations about how these typologies can be used to help generate and develop research questions.

The issue of what makes a question 'researchable' is the focus of Chapter 3. The chapter starts by differentiating questions that are answerable 'in principle' from those that are answerable 'in practice'. It highlights the impact of time and other resources on the kinds of questions that can be addressed in a particular context and emphasizes the importance of being realistic about what can be achieved in a single research project. The ways in which language can be used to 'bound' the limits of your research questions are explored in some detail, as are the ways in which questions can be ordered and structured most effectively. The importance of keeping research questions as brief and precise as possible is also discussed alongside advice on how this can be achieved.

Chapter 4 examines the relationship between research questions, research design and methods of data collection and analysis. The importance of starting with research questions is stressed, and the dangers of 'methods-led' research are outlined. Particular attention is paid to the process operationalizing the concepts that are central to your research project and developing and using suitable indictors.

The final chapter looks at *answering* research questions. It examines the structure of arguments used to link evidence to conclusions and introduces the idea of 'warranting' claims. The role that a warrant plays in linking evidence and conclusions is explained, as is the way in which a warrant demonstrates the principles of reasoning underlying an argument. The book ends by discussing the importance of considering alternative explanations for your research findings.

1 Where do research ideas come from?

CURIOSITY AND SURPRISE: THE BASIS OF INQUIRY

> Questions are everywhere; all you have to do is observe and be curious
>
> Graziano and Raulin (2004, p. 57)

Research should always be driven by curiosity. Genuine curiosity is characterized not only by being open-minded about the *answers* to particular questions but also about the *questions* that might be asked in the first place (Lewins 1992). While this may seem to be a very obvious point to make, it is all too easy for researchers to stray from a position of curiosity. Such lapses, however, are almost always detrimental to the conduct of high-quality research.

In order to conduct a research project, it is vital that you have an interest in the topic you are investigating. However, being interested in a topic and *having an interest* in the results of an investigation are very different. If you have something to gain or lose based on the outcome of a particular piece of research, you are unlikely to be the best person to conduct that research, as you may prefer certain outcomes or findings over others. Whilst it is impossible for a researcher to have no impact at all on the course of a research project, it is important to be vigilant against the influence of your beliefs and preferences on the research process. This is particularly important at the beginning of your research when choosing topics to investigate and developing your research questions.

You can still be genuinely curious *and* have ideas about the answers to your research questions, however. In fact, it is important to have a clear idea about the *type* of answers that are possible given the nature of your questions, and it can even be useful to make predictions about what the results *might* look like. As is explained in Chapter 2, this is exactly how hypotheses are generated. What is important is that you do not *pre-empt* the outcome of your research and that you are prepared to be surprised by your findings (Pole & Lampard 2002). This may mean writing up results that were entirely unexpected or even findings that might be considered 'undesirable'.

Being open-minded about the questions you investigate and the results of your research is not always as easy as it first appears. Academic communities can be quite conservative in some respects and 'habits of thought' within particular disciplines or subject areas can lead to research becoming formulaic and repetitive (Sellitz et al. 1965). It is certainly the case that researchers asking new or different questions, which may require the use of new or innovate research methods, will attract a greater degree of scrutiny than those who conduct studies that are very similar to those that preceded them. Research findings that are unexpected or surprising are certainly not treated the same as results that confirm the *status quo* in a particular area. They can, however, be very important and play a significant role in advancing our understanding of a particular topic (Labovitz & Hagedorn 1971, Campbell et al. 1982).

While a 'curious' approach to inquiry is to be encouraged, research cannot be conducted on this basis alone. An investigation cannot be based on 'idle' curiosity, as this will result in a haphazard research design and weaken the value and usefulness of any findings. Curiosity must be applied in a 'systematic' and 'disciplined' manner (Lewins 1992, Graziano & Raulin 2004). The following four chapters will take you through the steps required to move from your initial ideas for a study, through the formulation of a set of clear and well-structured research questions, to a point at which you are ready to start constructing a research design that can effectively address those questions.

In order to use your curiosity more effectively, you might find the following steps helpful at the beginning of your investigation:

- Think imaginatively about the kind of questions that could be asked in your area of interest.

- Try not to be too constrained by previous work in your field, either in terms of questions or methods.
- Think about the types of answers that particular questions can produce but keep an open mind about what your findings might be.

THE ROLE OF THE LITERATURE: KNOWING THE FIELD

Research does not, or *should* not take place in a vacuum. It is important to be aware as to how your study fits into the broader picture, in terms of previous empirical work, theoretical ideas, and recent policy and practice, as research that is conducted without considering these contexts risks being repetitive, irrelevant or of little value. As Lewins (1992, p. 8) suggests, 'to be scientific is to accept that the practice of asking questions builds on previous research or answers to other questions, and is therefore capable of contributing to an accumulation of what we call knowledge'.

The literature in a particular area can be a valuable source of ideas and a useful guide to what is already known about a topic. It can help establish the significance of a study by setting it in a wider context and linking it to related debates and can also provide guidance as to possible research methods and designs (Denscombe 2002). Most commentators agree that researchers should engage with the existing literature to some extent before proceeding too far with a study.

However, there is much less agreement about *how* and *when* different types of literature should be used while planning a research project. I have already suggested that researchers, especially – but not exclusively – those with relatively little experience, can be unduly influenced by existing thinking in an area. This can be restricting and may stifle innovation and creativity. It is difficult to imagine a useful study that does not engage with existing literature at all, but exposure to the literature can be something of a double-edged sword. In the following discussion, five issues relating to the relationship between the literature and research questions are raised alongside suggestions for how to resolve these tensions. These issues relate to the following questions:

- Should I start by reviewing the literature or start with a research question?
- Where do I start reading and when should I stop reading?
- What counts as a 'gap' in our knowledge and how large does it need to be?
- What makes research 'original' and how important is originality?
- To what extent should I be influenced by previous findings and theories?

Starting with the literature or starting with a question

One of the problems you might face at the beginning of a research project is whether you should formulate research questions *before* reviewing the literature or use the literature to generate ideas for research questions. This is something of a 'Catch 22' situation because while the literature review can help identify interesting and topical questions, it is difficult to know where to start reading if you do not have a question to act as a guide (Hudson-Barr 2005).

If you are required to conduct a research project but have only a vague notion of what you want to investigate, the existing literature can be enormously helpful in identifying key issues in a particular area. If you are interested in how people make choices about their educational and occupational careers, for example, it will be relatively straightforward to find journal articles, research reports and policy documents relating to this topic. This can be done by searching bibliographic databases (either online or using CD-ROMs), asking teaching staff or academic colleagues or simply by browsing in the relevant section of your library. Once you have found and identified a small number of key texts, you can use the bibliographies to track down more literature in the area. The problem you will then face is when to *stop* reading and start formulating your own research questions (see below).

If you have absolutely no idea about what you want to research; however, you will not know where to start looking and any literature search will be both aimless and time consuming (Andrews 2003). It is important that you have at least *some* idea about what you want to research before beginning to review the literature. The more focused and developed your idea is, the more it will guide you during the literature search.

There are several ways you can generate ideas for research topics if you cannot think of an area of interest straightaway. Looking through newspapers can be helpful as it will give you an idea of the kind of issues that are currently topical. Most broadsheet papers (such as the *Independent, Guardian* or *Times*) provide coverage of social policy and social problems, and they also publish supplements dedicated to particular areas, including education, media, society, politics and business. These supplements provide in-depth coverage of issues in these areas and can be very helpful in generating research ideas. Magazines covering social issues, such as the *New Statesman,* the *Times Educational Supplement,* the *Economist* and the *New Internationalist* can also serve the same purpose. And as newspapers and magazines are now available to access online you can even follow up any interesting issues using the search tools available on the newspapers' websites. Any relevant articles can also be used in your literature review to demonstrate that your research relates directly to contemporary concerns.

Watching the television news, current affairs programmes or documentaries can also focus your attention on particular issues. Radio broadcasts on stations such as BBC Radio 4 can serve a similar purpose. These sources will be more difficult to use in a literature review (although programme transcripts are sometimes available) but will be no less useful in generating ideas for research.

Another source of ideas for research is the courses you have previously taken or are currently studying. Going through your course handbook, lecture notes or recommended texts may spark your interest in a particular topic. Asking your lecturers or seminar tutors may also be helpful. They will be knowledgeable about current debates in an area and should also have a clear idea about what you will be able to achieve given the time available to you.

Spending time thinking about research questions at the very beginning of your research will certainly save you time when it comes to reviewing the literature. This is particularly important if you are expected to complete your research project in a relatively short space of time, as is often the case for undergraduate or masters level degrees. Being as clear as you can be about what you want to research *before* you start reading in-depth is important, as it is easy to spend a great deal of time 'bogged-down' in the literature if you are not really sure what you are looking for. You will probably find that your questions change to a certain extent once you are familiar with previous research findings and key debates in a particular area, but try not to worry about this when you are initially thinking about ideas for a study. What is important is that you have a sufficiently clear idea of what topic you want to research in order to provide direction for your review of the literature.

Unlike many students, practitioner-researchers, action-researchers and those conducting 'applied' or 'policy' research will often have very clear ideas about what problems and questions they wish to address. However, being clear about the focus of an investigation does not mean that reviewing the literature is unnecessary. Research questions often need to be refined, and it is always a good idea to link your particular study to related theoretical ideas, substantive findings, and debates about policy and practice. Such links can only usually be made by reviewing the literature in these areas.

Key Points

- Don't start your literature search without *some* idea of the topic you want to investigate.
- Use the media, course notes or discussions with academic staff to generate initial ideas.
- Spending time thinking about your questions will save time during your literature review.

Where to start reading and when to stop reading

Even when they have identified a topic to investigate, in my experience many students often find it difficult to find a place to *begin* reading. And once they have found their way into the literature they often find it difficult to stop reading and move on to the next stage of the research.

Because research is published in a variety of forms, with different publications often being aimed at different audiences, it is not surprising that inexperienced researchers find it difficult to identify the publications that will be most useful to them. Even within a well-defined substantive area, the vast range of literature available can seem bewildering.

One of the best ways to navigate the literature is to seek some expert advice. If you have been allocated a research supervisor, they will usually be familiar with the area you are studying and able to point to some key publications. If your research is unsupervised, you may find it helpful to approach a knowledgeable member of your department or organization for advice. But do not be afraid to venture beyond your own backyard. Researchers working in other departments or even in other institutions will often respond helpfully to a simple email request for information on suggested reading. It is advisable to seek expert advice *before* starting your literature search, if at all possible, as this will minimize the time it takes to locate relevant publications.

If such advice is not available, particular types of publication can serve as natural starting points for a literature review. Specialist, peer-reviewed journals are a good place to start, especially if you have a fairly clear idea of what topic you are interested in. Journals vary in the degree to which they specialize, however, and will be more or less useful depending on their coverage of your research topic. Even within a particular substantive area, there are large numbers of journals, ranging from the very general to the very specialized. In the area in which I conduct most of my research – education – there are literally hundreds of different journals, serving different purposes and aimed at different audiences. While publications such as the *Oxford Review of Education*, *Research Papers in Education* and the *British Journal of Education* may be widely read and are very prestigious, their breadth of coverage means that only a very small proportion of articles they publish are likely to coincide with my particular research interests. Other journals such as *Gender and Education* and *Race, Ethnicity and Education* focus on particular issues but still cover a wide range of substantive areas. At the other end of the scale are journals dedicated to very narrow areas of inquiry, such as the *Journal of Music Teacher Education* and *Children's Literature in Education*.

The type of journal that is of most use will depend on the extent to which your research questions have been developed and refined. If your questions are relatively clear and well defined you are more likely to be able to locate specialist journals focusing on similar or related topics. Students with more vague ideas about what they want to research may find that browsing through some of the more general journals sparks their interest in a particular area. However, while there are literally hundreds of journals published in each social science discipline, you should not rely on their being a specialist journal that corresponds exactly to your needs. Some substantive areas are better catered for than others and, even when a relevant journal exists, you are unlikely to be able to access it unless it is available in your library. You should bear in mind, however, that a good literature review will cover material from a wide range of sources and should not be restricted to articles in a few specialist publications. At some point you will need to broaden your search beyond these journals.

Another way of locating relevant literature, and perhaps a better one for those with less well-developed research ideas, is to look for introductory texts. These can range from the very general, such as *Sport, Culture and Society* (Jarvie 2006) to more specialized texts such as *Sport and Social Exclusion* (Collins 2002). These texts are designed to familiarize readers with key issues in a particular area and can be a good starting place for those wishing to narrow down their initial area of interest. Equally useful are edited collections, and these, 'readers', are books that focus on a particular theme or substantive area, with each chapter written by different authors. They collect together the work of a number of different researchers in a particular field and can offer an overview of work in that area. An example of such an edited collection would be *Fighting Fans: Football Hooliganism as a World Phenomenon* (Dunning et al. 2002). Larger edited collections, often called 'handbooks' are also available in some areas, the *Handbook of Sport Studies* (Coakley & Dunning 2002) being one example. These sometimes span several volumes but can be useful for assessing the 'state of the art' in a particular field in a relatively short space of time. Like journals, however, readers and handbooks vary in the degree to which they specialize. While recognizing the limits of what is available, you should try to find publications that are appropriate to the stage your ideas have reached.

Some writers advocate delaying exposure to the literature until later in the research process. While there is considerable debate surrounding 'grounded theory', an approach to research originally proposed by Glaser and Strauss (1967), some researchers advocating this method suggest deliberately delaying the literature review until after themes and concepts have emerged from the data. Instead, literature is introduced later in the research process and treated as additional data (Punch 1998). This approach is intended to reduce the influence of existing theories and explanations on the researcher's interpretation of his or her own data.

Other commentators argue that those conducting 'applied' research need not concern themselves with *particular aspects* of the existing literature. Tymms and Taylor Fitz-Gibbon (2002) argue that applied research is more likely to be impeded than aided by a preoccupation with theory, and that research into practical problems can be conducted perfectly well (or perhaps even better) with minimal theoretical knowledge (see also Scriven 1998). It should be noted, however, that these authors are not suggesting that a review of the existing literature be completely bypassed, only that researchers need not concern themselves greatly with the various *theoretical* debates that accompany particular areas of inquiry.

These approaches, however, are risky for inexperienced researchers and may not even be possible for students conducting research as part of undergraduate or masters degrees. Detailed proposals for research projects, including summaries of the theoretical background and relevant substantive literature, are often required as part of the assessment process. And funding bodies that sponsor postgraduate students, such as the *Economic and Social Research Council*, require similar documents as part of their studentship funding application processes. New researchers are probably best sticking to a more conventional approach, especially if their course requirements dictate early engagement with the literature.

Your engagement with the literature may vary depending on the origin of your research questions. When the research questions have emerged from professional, organizational or institutional contexts (see below) the research is often of a particularly 'applied' character, focusing on particular problems of immediate practical relevance. In such cases, the research questions are often well defined and have been formulated before the literature review has even begun. In these studies the literature provides a 'background resource' for research rather than acting as the stimulus for the research. Some questions, however, are more theoretical in nature and arise from within the literature itself. As such questions usually arise from familiarity with the academic literature in an area, in such cases it is necessary to conduct some kind of review of the literature *before* meaningful questions can be formulated.

Most writers argue that some degree of exposure to the literature is a vital element of any investigation, regardless of the origin of the research questions. While the precise role of the literature will vary depending on the type of research questions you propose to address, it is important not to exaggerate the differences between 'applied' and 'theoretical' research. There is no firm dividing line between the two (Hakim 2000) and most studies cannot easily be fitted into either category (Graziano & Raulin 2004). Solving practical problems requires background knowledge, some of which originates from theoretical research, and theoretical issues inevitably become evident once practical problems are explored and elaborated (Hammersley & Atkinson 1995). And the findings of even the most theoretically led studies can have practical applications, even if these are not anticipated at the outset.

The literature can be useful for making links between 'applied' and 'theoretical' concerns. Questions arising directly from practical concerns *should*, where possible, be linked to relevant theories in order for the findings to be transferred to other problems (Sellitz et al. 1965). In this way it is possible to move 'upwards in generality and abstraction' in order to connect specific research questions to more general issues (Punch 1998, p. 35).

Punch (1998) recommends two different methods of arriving at research questions and describes the ways in which these can be connected to the wider literature. If specific research questions have already been identified (as is common in applied research) it is helpful to first link these with more general questions, which in turn can be connected with a wider area of study. For example, research aiming to discover the reasons young people give for drinking alcohol could be linked to research on young people's lifestyle choices and the literature in the area of drug use more generally. Evidence from such a study could also inform theoretical debates about decision-making and risk-taking.

If you have not yet identified specific questions but are interested in a particular *topic*, you must first try to move towards a set of general questions or issues, from which specific research questions can then be derived. You might be interested in the areas of crime and gender and want to combine these topics in your research. This is a very broad area, however, and unless any particular questions immediately spring to mind, exploring the literature might help focus your interest in a particular topic. While this is a topic I am completely unfamiliar with, a quick search of my library's electronic catalogue revealed three relatively recent text books in this area (Walklate 2004, Heimer 2006, Morash 2006), as well as more than ten similar, older texts. I also found a slightly dated government report on the topic (Home Office 1997). Browsing these publications could help you not only narrow down your area of interest but also locate more specialist literature. You might, for example, decide that you are most interested in women offenders. You could follow up the references provided in the text books you have read and perhaps even conduct a more focused search in the library. A quick search of my library revealed at least one recent text specializing in this area (Farrington 2004). As you continue to narrow your topic you will find that you can be more purposeful in directing your search.

There are very good practical reasons for not delaying a review of the literature until relatively late in the research. It may be the case that the questions that you have raised have already been answered by previous research, either in the same context or one which is sufficiently similar for the findings to be transferred. 'Wilful neglect' of the literature risks 're-inventing the wheel'; not a desirable outcome for those wishing to make a contribution to knowledge. The degree to which research should be 'new' or 'original' is not a simple matter, however, and deciding whether a set of research questions cover a sufficient amount of new territory is not straightforward. These issues are addressed over the course of the next two sections of this chapter, where the notion of 'gaps' in existing knowledge and the importance of 'originality' in research are both explored.

One of the most difficult decisions during the course of a research project is when to stop reading. 'Disengaging' with the literature can cause a great deal of anxiety as it represents moving from the comfortable world of the ideas of others into the uncertain world of your own research. As always, supervisors or experienced colleagues should be able to offer advice in this area. An important point to remember, however, is that you *never* completely disengage with the literature. While you may read more intensively at the beginning of your project you should carry on reading throughout the research process, whenever you have time. Many researchers suggest that researchers should return to the literature repeatedly over the course of a project (Jorgenson 1989). The development of research questions thus becomes an 'iterative' task, with the researcher moving back and forth between the literature and the evolving questions and research design (Marshall & Rossman 1999). Bearing this in mind may ease your anxiety both about 'finishing' the review of literature and moving from your initial research questions on to the next stages of your project.

Summary
- If it is available, get expert help on where to begin reading.
- Specialist journals, general texts and edited collections are good places to start your literature review.
- It is probably best to explore the literature at the beginning of your project, rather than leave it until later on.
- Try not to worry about moving on from the literature or research questions: you will revisit both on a regular basis.

Not re-inventing the wheel: what counts as a 'gap' and how big does it need to be?

Reviewing the existing literature in an area can serve several functions. One of the most important is to identify what is already known about a topic in order to avoid 're-inventing the wheel' by researching a particular question that has already been answered (Cozby et al. 1989). This is not to say that you cannot replicate a particular study – replication plays a valuable role in scientific inquiry – but in order to do so you would at the very least need to be aware of the study you wished to replicate! The key point here is that it is senseless and wasteful to conduct a study to answer research questions that have already been satisfactorily addressed. Indeed, one of the defining characteristics of scientific inquiry is that it is cumulative; each new study builds on the findings of previous ones (Lewins 1992).

One of the most commonly suggested ways of generating ideas for research questions is by identifying a 'gap' in the existing literature (Mason 1996). In order to do this, some knowledge of the literature is obviously required. But as it is unreasonable to expect *any* researcher – let alone a student – to have a truly comprehensive knowledge of an area, identifying gaps is not necessarily a straightforward task.

Finding a gap in the literature can be quite a subtle activity. It is sometimes difficult for novice researchers to identify new areas of inquiry, as recognizing gaps or new questions is a skill that must be learned and practised before it becomes second nature. It may not be the case that a gap is immediately obvious, and discussions with colleagues, supervisors or other students may help beginning researchers locate potential areas for study.

Advanced researchers often start by identifying questions that may have been addressed in previous research but have not been answered 'thoroughly or even correctly' (Booth et al. 2003, p. 51). Contradictions, inconsistencies and incomplete explanations can all provide good starting points for research (Greer 1978). Such a strategy might seem too ambitious or risky to be attempted by a student or novice researcher, but it should not be completely ruled out as a possible source of ideas. It is important to make sure that new questions do actually address a genuine deficiency, absence or omission, however, as 'countless research papers have aimed to refute a point that no writer has ever made' (Booth et al. 2003, p. 69).

My students often express concern that the questions they wish to address are too minor. Most of those who have supervised research students would no doubt agree that the opposite is much more likely to be the case and that students are prone to over-ambition in the initial stages of planning a study. The cumulative nature of inquiry means that researchers spend most of their professional lives investigating very specific issues and, because they are limited by the skills, time and other resources available to them. Beginning researchers can sometimes feel that the problems they are working on are insignificant. This is very rarely the case, however, as along with others working in the same field their research will be contributing to the process of answering much larger questions, with much more obvious implications and importance (Medawar 1979). However, while researchers may wish to contribute to the 'big' questions, their own projects must be guided by more modest, specific research questions (Black 1993).

Key Points

- It is important to know the literature in your area so that you don't 're-invent the wheel'.
- Finding a 'gap' in the literature can be one way of generating ideas for research.
- Don't worry about the focus of your study being too minor. It is more likely that it is over-ambitious.

Originality

Before discussing influence and originality it is necessary to point out that some research projects need not be original at all. Most undergraduate dissertations are tests of students' competence in research, rather than opportunities to make an original contribution to knowledge. Undergraduate students should not worry too much about the extent to which their research is original or fills a gap in the literature. Their primary concern should be with formulating research questions that can be addressed using the limited time and resources available, and choosing an appropriate research design. Because of this, they may wish to skip the rest of this section.

Postgraduate students, however, may be required to incorporate some element of originality into their research. The extent to which masters theses need to be original will vary, but it is usually assumed that doctoral research will be 'original' in some respect. 'Originality' is a problematic term in relation to social research, however. It is not clear that any study is entirely 'original', in the commonsense understanding of the term, or that even replication studies are unoriginal. Some commentators have suggested that 'originality' has a different meaning in relation to research compared to common-place usage of the term, although how the term can usefully mean something different in relation to research is unclear. Despite these problems, students are routinely instructed to ensure that their research is 'original' in some respect, often because of the requirements written into research degree specifications.

It has been suggested that a study can be considered original if it makes a novel contribution in one or more of the following four areas: topic, method, data or analysis (Denscombe 2002). Most obviously, if a study investigates a particular substantive area that has not been researched previously, the research will be original by virtue of this fact alone. This would also be the case if new questions were asked in an area that was already well researched. Additionally, research can be considered original if an innovative research design or new method of data collection or analysis is used, regardless of the topic of investigation or questions posed. However, Denscombe (2002) also suggests that any research with 'new' data is also original.

Denscombe's (2002) last criterion for originality hints at the reason why the goal of originality is something of a straw target in social research, as the majority of research projects include some data that could be considered 'new'. Although it is possible to imagine exceptions, almost all data that are collected in fieldwork or laboratory settings are 'new' data, in the sense of not having been collected beforehand and so would confer a degree of originality to a study. Even data collected as part of a 'replication' study would be considered to be new, as they would relate to different participants, in a different context and at a different point in time. Indeed, it has been argued that the basic concept of replication is problematic, even in the natural sciences (Collins 1985).

The only data that would not meet this criterion would be what are traditionally termed 'secondary' data – data that have been collected previously by other researchers for different purposes. However, in most social science disciplines (perhaps excluding economics) only a small minority of studies rely exclusively on secondary data, and the same analyses are rarely conducted on identical data sets (Smith 2008). The range and availability of these data mean that opportunities for conducting original analyses are almost innumerable.

Because of these issues, it is probably not very helpful for postgraduate students to spend a great deal of time worrying about the extent to which their study will or will not be original. However, this reassurance is not intended to encourage complacency or suggest that imaginative and innovative approaches to research are not to be encouraged. It is certainly the case that too many research projects rely on similar approaches and entire fields of research can easily become stuck in 'ruts', both in relation to the type of questions asked and the kind of research designs routinely employed (Campbell et al. 1982, Taylor 2002). Researchers should always aim to be innovative but, as is discussed in Chapter 4, the most important consideration should always be the data that are required to address a particular question. Innovation for innovation's sake is not necessarily desirable in social research.

As with many such issues, the best advice for novice researchers is to seek expert guidance from a supervisor or a more experienced colleague. This solution is not without its drawbacks, however, as those with the longest histories in an area are also the most likely to be constrained by the conventions within the field. Listening to the advice of others can be very valuable, but researchers should ultimately rely on their own judgement when making decisions about the direction of their research.

Key Points

- Undergraduate students need not worry about the extent to which their research is 'original' – they should concentrate on demonstrating their competence in conducting research.
- Originality can take many forms, including innovation in relation to methods of data collection and analysis as well as asking new questions.
- It is difficult to imagine studies that are completely 'unoriginal' and even doctoral students should not be overly concerned about this criterion.

Influence

An issue closely related to originality is the degree to which researchers should be influenced by existing work in their area of interest. It is very easy to follow current fashions when choosing topics for research but several commentators advise against this (e.g. Medawar 1979, Campbell et al. 1982). The importance of questions or topics should not be judged by how often they occur in the literature, as some of the more popular questions may be studied simply because they are straightforward to research rather than because it is important that they are answered. Other, more significant, questions may be neglected because addressing them would be very challenging. Take care to recognize, however, that particular questions may have been ignored simply because they are unresearchable (see Chapters 2 and 3).

Existing research in an area should be treated with caution in terms of its influence on the choice of a particular issue or question for investigation. There is a danger that reviewing previous studies can lead researchers to be too derivative in their question formulation, maintaining the status quo in what might already be an area of inquiry characterized by conservative thinking. Substantive areas can quickly become characterized by 'habits of thought' (Sellitz et al. 1965, p. 31) which can work against the development of new approaches or perspectives (Punch 1998). The traditional modes of thought in particular areas, or even disciplines, extend beyond the choice of *what* to study into decisions about *how* to conduct an investigation. New researchers must beware of being 'imprisoned' by previous approaches to investigating a topic (Robson 1993). Do not be afraid to use new and innovative research designs or methods of data collection and analysis, so long as you are confident they are appropriate and that you have the ability to carry them out.

The fact that certain kinds of questions logically lead to the use of particular methods (see Chapter 4) does not necessarily mean that the most commonly used methods are the most appropriate for a particular type of investigation. Unfortunately, it is all too common for researchers to use methods of data collection and analysis that they are most comfortable with rather than those that are best suited to the objectives of their research. Neither is it the case that the existence of a tradition of using particular research methods means that that there is no room for innovation or creative thinking in a research design.

> **Key Points**
> - The importance of questions or topics should *not* be judged by how often they arise in the literature.
> - Paying too much attention to previous studies can lead to derivative and conservative research.
> - You must pay attention to previous studies but should not be afraid to ask new questions or use innovative research methods.

The questions posed at the beginning of this chapter have been addressed in the preceding discussions. The following sections go on to examine the roles of different types of literature in the generation and development of research questions. The role of theory is considered first.

THE ROLE OF THEORY

It is commonly suggested that theoretical ideas can provide a useful source of research questions. In fact, some academics spend their entire careers engaging with theoretical questions, happy to leave the testing of their theories to others. Students are often told that they must link their research projects to wider theoretical debates and may be encouraged to think about the ways in which their research contributes to theoretical understanding in a particular area. But what exactly do we mean by theory? And how can it help you generate research questions? In this section, the idea of theory and its relationship to research questions is explored. The following two sections examine two different ways in which theory can be used to generate ideas for research questions.

What is theory?

> Theories are nets to catch what we call 'the world': to rationalise, explain and master it.
>
> (Popper 1959: 2002, pp. 37–8)

At the very start of this discussion it is important to point out that 'theory' is a contested term. While many people write about 'theory', they are not always referring to exactly same thing, and the meaning of the term varies between the natural sciences, humanities and social sciences (Abrahamson 1983). I will try to argue here, however, that some definitions of 'theory' are more useful than others. For those conducting empirical research, the most important characteristics of a theory are that it is an idea that is

- abstract
- explanatory
- testable.

An idea is 'abstract' if it is applicable to a variety of different situations or phenomena, rather than only a single event or occurrence. A theory of social stratification, for example, would seek to explain why lots of different people find themselves in a number of socio-economic situations, at different times, rather than simply how one individual has ended up where they are at a particular moment. For readers who are unclear about this concept and require further clarification, Bulmer (1979, p. 21) provides a very clear and detailed discussion of what is meant by 'abstraction'.

The second characteristic is that theories should be explanatory. Continuing with the example above, a theory of stratification should be able to *explain* why some people move between social strata and others do not. It should seek to go beyond describing how society is currently stratified, to explain exactly why it is like this and even predict how it might change.

Lastly, theories should be empirically testable. This means that we should be able to see how well they work in practice by collecting and analysing relevant data. This is perhaps *the* most important characteristic of a theory. While some commentators have questioned the extent to which theories should be either explanatory or abstracted (e.g. Shaw & Costanzo 1970, Bulmer 1979) the idea that a theory should be able to be tested empirically is central to most definitions (see Cozby et al. 1989). A theory that cannot be tested is of little use, as it is impossible to assess the extent to which it matches up with reality. It is unusual for whole theories to be tested by one piece of research, however. It is much more likely that a series of 'hypotheses' are logically deduced from a theory and then tested individually (see Chapter 2).

For the purposes of most students conducting research, it is sufficient to view theories as explanations, formulated at an abstract level, that are able to be tested via empirical research. They often, but do not always, seek to explain the relationship between two or more phenomena, with the goal of allowing us to make predictions about future events.

Theory testing and theory generation

Many researchers have argued that, to be meaningful, research questions should be linked to theoretical issues (e.g. Campbell et al. 1982, Popper 1972, Bradley 2001). Research that addresses wider theoretical concerns is much less likely to be dismissed as 'trivial' and will also appeal to a wider audience (Hammersley & Atkinson 1995, Mason 1996). But what are the best ways of doing this? And how can theory be used to help formulate research questions?

Theories can be related to research questions in two main ways. They can be tested, with the research questions relating to their ability to help us understand a particular aspect of the social world. Alternatively, gaps in existing theories can be identified and research can aim to generate theory in order to make up for this absence. These two approaches are often described as 'theory testing' and 'theory generation'.

In 'theory testing' ('theory-first') studies, hypotheses are derived from a theory and are then subjected to empirical testing. (The relationship between research questions and hypotheses is explored in detail in Chapter 2.) In contrast, the aim of 'theory generation' (or 'theory-after') research is to produce theories as the result of the investigation (Punch 1998).

Whether you decide to adopt one of these approaches, and which one is appropriate, will depend on many factors. The most important consideration, however, is likely to be the extent to which theories have already been developed in your area of interest (Sellitz et al. 1965, Punch 1998). As previously mentioned, you will obviously need to conduct a search of the literature and engage in some preliminary reading before you will be able to decide whether your topic of inquiry might be suited to either theory testing or theory generation.

In contrast to the suggestions made by some authors (either explicitly or otherwise) it is not necessary to conduct 'qualitative' research in order to generate theory, nor is it the case that theories can only be tested in 'quantitative' studies (Hammersley & Atkinson 1995). Whether you generate or test theories (or even do both) will depend on the topic, context and practical circumstances of the research (Punch 1998). The deciding factor is the extent to which theory has been developed in that particular area, rather than the research methods used.

One of my current undergraduate students, for example, has decided to use a theory testing approach in his research project. He was interested in finding out the reasons why some students take 'academic' A-levels and others take 'vocational' A-levels. After doing some reading in the area, he found that many studies of educational choice referred to Pierre Bourdieu's concept of 'cultural capital' (Bourdieu 1986). He decided to see if this theoretical concept could help explain why students opted for different types of qualification in the same subject area. As is discussed in Chapter 4, this concept is far from unproblematic but it provided the stimulus for this student to formulate some interesting research questions and attempt to test an element of a wider theory in a particular context.

My doctoral research was also in the area of educational choice (see White 2007). In contrast, however, I was unhappy with the limitations of the theories of choice that were popular at the time (including those using Bourdieu's concepts) and attempted to generate a new theoretical model of decision-making using the data collected in my study. While it is easier to make a theoretical contribution in areas where conceptual work is sparse, the *quality* of existing theories can be as important as their *quantity* in terms of fostering interest in theory generation. There were plenty of well-established theories of choice in existence at the time of my study but I did not feel that they would be very useful in the context of my research.

The theoretical literature can be a useful source of research questions. However, while postgraduate students may be sufficiently confident to either test or generate theories, only the most ambitious undergraduate students are likely to attempt either of these in their research. Those conducting research as part of an undergraduate programme should think carefully before taking either route, and should ensure that they have adequate support and advice from a supervisor or experienced researcher. Testing theory, while not without its difficulties, tends to be easier than generating new theories and may be a more realistic option for those conducting research for the first time. It is important to remember that you can *link* your research to theoretical ideas without having to either test theories or generate new ones. This is a more important consideration for most students, especially those with little previous research experience.

Key Points

- Theory can provide a good starting point for research.
- Some research aims to test existing theories, other studies aim to generate new theoretical ideas.
- Either approach can be challenging and should be approached with caution by inexperienced researchers.
- It is important to link your research to theory even if your research is not inspired by theoretical ideas.

'PRACTICAL' STIMULI FOR RESEARCH QUESTIONS

As mentioned earlier in this chapter, some ideas for research can emerge from practical, rather than theoretical concerns. This is often the case for practitioner-researchers, who usually want to research issues directly related to their work. Students and researchers who are interested in public policy may also be interested in how particular pieces of legislation work in practice, however. Both policy and practice can stimulate interest in particular areas or topics, and can in turn generate interesting research questions.

The policy context and social problems

Policy can provide a useful starting point for generating ideas for research. Libraries have traditionally held important policy documents and nowadays it is relatively simple to download recent policy documents using the internet. Policy research is often focused on the extent to which legislation has ameliorated particular 'social problems', and so its salience can be immediately obvious (Greer 1978, Blumer 1979, Robson 1993). Because it addresses issues perceived as important by politicians, officials and/or the public, research of this kind is relatively easy to justify, an important consideration for students seeking postgraduate studentships or those applying for other kinds of research funding.

While policy research is often concerned with legislation enacted at a national level by government departments, it is important to remember that policy is also made at regional, local and institutional levels. Policy formulated and implemented at *any* level can provide stimulus for interesting research questions, and researchers with limited time and resources – such as undergraduate and masters students – may find that polices applied on a relatively small scale provide the most suitable opportunities for investigation. I was involved in a research project researching school admissions, for example, which examined policies operating at the national, local authority and institutional levels (see White et al. 2001). It was possible to investigate all three contexts in which the policies were applied simply because the project was externally funded, well resourced and conducted over a number of years. However, *any one* of these contexts would have provided enough scope for an undergraduate or masters research project. In fact, for most small-scale projects, the policy documents themselves would have constituted sufficient data for a very interesting study.

As policies are usually accompanied by supporting documentation, these texts can serve as a useful starting point for generating research questions (Marshall & Rossman 1999, Bradley 2001). In some cases their use may go beyond the initial formulation of questions, as the documents themselves may be valuable as data in their own right. This was the case in the research described directly above and, indeed, some research is concerned solely with the analysis of policy literature.

Whatever the starting point for research, the potential policy implications for any findings should not be ignored. Research is never conducted in a 'policy vacuum' (Pole & Lampard 2002) and in the same way as theory is drawn into even the most practically oriented study there can be unexpected policy implications arising from all kinds of inquiry (Hammersley & Atkinson 1995). As was discussed earlier in relation to theory, linking your research project to contemporary policy is desirable, even if your research questions originated elsewhere.

As policies are often concerned with addressing particular aspects of social problems, it is not surprising that the two are frequently discussed together. However, social problems themselves can constitute a rich source of ideas for research questions, regardless of their relationship to particular policy initiatives. Investigating the 'incidence and persistence' of a problem can be particularly valuable (Marshall & Rossman 1999) and there will certainly never be a shortage of problems to investigate (Robson 1993). The outcomes of such research would clearly have implications for any future policy initiatives at many levels.

A useful indicator of the policies and social problems is the amount of coverage they receive in the media. Browsing broadsheet newspapers can be a good strategy for students looking for ideas for a research project, as the most topical policies and problems will usually be addressed in some detail. Tabloid newspapers, while short on detail, can serve as a different kind of indicator of public (or at least media) concern. Documents relating to specific policies can usually be downloaded from government department websites once an interesting area of policy has been identified, and there are journals such as *Health Policy, Criminology and Public Policy* and the *Journal of Education Policy* that deal specifically with policy-oriented research.

The abundance of information in the area means that policy can be a good starting point for research topics. Social problems are equally fertile areas of investigation, and inquiries into either area can be easily defended in terms of their relevance and importance. Another area that can generate research questions, and one closely linked to policy and social problems, focuses on the practise of professionals working in various settings. These types of questions, and the research that attempts to address them, are often characterized as 'applied' in nature. They are discussed in more detail in the following section.

Key Points

- Research questions can originate in practical concerns rather than the academic literature.
- Policy formulated at all levels can provide ideas for research questions, or even be used as a source of data.
- 'Social problems' can also generate ideas for research projects.
- Media coverage, government websites and specialist journals can all be used as indicators of current concerns about policy and social problems.

'Applied' research

'Applied' research is a term used to describe a variety of investigative approaches including action research, evaluation research and practitioner research. Applied research questions tend to originate in the world of professional practice rather than in academic settings. They are primarily concerned with addressing a practical problem of immediate concern, rather than contributing to wider social scientific debates (Sellitz et al. 1965, Abrahamson 1983, Hakim 2000, Milton 2000). They are often set in organizational or institutional contexts (Punch 1998) and are concerned with specific sites or populations (Marshall & Rossman 1999). 'Applied research' tends to be carried out in areas such as health, education, social work and criminal justice, although it is by no means restricted to these contexts.

Given their proximity to the practice setting and the centrality of practice problems to their professional lives, it is unsurprising that many practitioners are keen to conduct research. Autobiography often plays a key role in generating research ideas (Platt 1976) and this is particularly the case in applied settings (Marshall & Rossman 1999). Indeed, ideas for applied research often originate from practitioners, even when they are not directly involved in conducting the research. Examining present practice or beliefs about 'good practice' can be good starting points for research (Ferns & Riedel 1995, Macintyre 2000).

For those not already familiar with the problems encountered in a practice setting, it may be useful to seek advice from those with practical experience in the field (Sellitz et al. 1965). It is vital to have input from the relevant professionals, who should also be intimately involved in the formulation of research questions (Mullen 2002). If you were conducting research into the careers of persistent offenders, for example, it may be necessary to consult with police officers, legal professionals, and staff from the prison and probation services in order to ascertain the most pressing areas of investigation.

One challenge inherent in applied research is transforming a practitioner's problem into a researchable problem (Soydan 2002). The nature of 'researchable' questions is examined in detail in Chapter 3, but it is sufficient for present purposes to raise the possibility that not all the problems and/or questions raised by practitioners can be adequately addressed through empirical inquiry. Questions regarding the differential educational attainment of various social groups has been of interest to teachers and researchers for many years, for example. While documenting these differences has been a relatively straightforward task, providing empirically grounded *explanations* for these differences has so far eluded researchers (Smith 2005).

Some commentators have noticed a tendency for applied research to be viewed as a less prestigious activity in comparison to 'pure' or 'basic' research, especially in academic circles. The successful and respected academics interviewed as part of Campbell et al.'s (1982) study certainly believed this to be the case, but few took this view themselves, the consensus being that too little applied research was being conducted at that time. Indeed, students and novice researchers certainly should not be deterred from attempting to solve practical problems through empirical research. As Robson (1993) suggests, there will never be a shortage of problems to address and there is often more funding available, both to students and professional researchers, to conduct applied research.

Key Points

- Applied research includes 'action research', 'evaluation research' and 'practitioner research'.
- Those already working in professional contexts may be particularly interested in researching issues relating to their work.
- It is important to realize that not all problems and questions raised in such contexts are 'researchable'.

SUMMARY

If you have read this whole chapter, you will hopefully have learned something about where research questions come from and the roles different stimuli play in generating research ideas. I started the chapter by making a case for the importance of both 'disciplined curiosity' and the capacity to be surprised by what you find out. As the epigraph at the very beginning suggests, if you are genuinely curious you will be able to get ideas for research simply by looking in the right places. Throughout this chapter I have suggested ways in which you can generate and refine research questions by using the existing literature and other sources of information. This advice should also help you find good places to start reviewing the literature.

In the next chapter the form and content of research questions are examined in greater detail. In order to get the most out of Chapter 2, it is best to have at least *some* idea about a topic or area of interest. If you have got to this stage you will be able to follow some of the advice provided to turn your initial ideas into research questions or refine your existing questions even further.

FURTHER READING

Both Dillon and Campbell et al. provide empirical evidence of the lack of attention given to research questions and the problems this creates:

Campbell, J.P., Daft, R.L. & Hulin, C.L. (1982) *What To Study: Generating and Developing Research Questions*. Beverley Hills, CA: Sage.

Dillon, J.T. (1983) 'The Use of Questions in Educational Research', *Educational Researcher*, 12 (9), pp. 19–24.

Detailed advice on reading and reviewing research publications can be found in

Locke, L.F., Silverman, S.J. & Spirduso, W.W. (2004) *Reading and Understanding Research*. 2nd Edn. Thousand Oaks, CA: Sage.

Abrahamson provides a clear discussion on the role of theory in social research:

Abrahamson, M. (1983) *Social Research Methods*. Englewood Cliffs, NJ: Prentice-Hall.

Bulmer's explanation of the concept of 'abstraction' is both clear and well illustrated:

Bulmer, M. (1979) 'Block 2A: Beginning Research', *DE304 Research Methods in Education and the Social Sciences*. Milton Keynes: Open University Press. ISBN 0 355 07436 7.

2 What makes a research question?

This chapter examines the nature of social scientific research questions. It explains why only certain types of question can be addressed by empirical research, and how thinking about what type of question you are asking can help develop, structure and order your research questions. The role of hypotheses in social research is also explained. The chapter begins by examining the important differences between research questions and other kinds of statements.

RESEARCH TOPICS, AIMS AND OBJECTIVES

Formulating good research questions can be very difficult. Students tend to be much more comfortable answering questions than asking them, perhaps because most programmes of education put more stress on the former (Dillon 1988). It is usually much easier to decide upon a topic or area of interest than it is to produce a set of well-structured and coherent questions. While topics and areas can be useful starting points for generating research ideas, they do not provide sufficient direction for conducting research. This is because, unlike questions, they are not sufficiently specific to inform you what data need to be collected or how these should be analysed. It is also the case that not every topic can be transformed into a feasible research project (Sellitz et al. 1965) and, in any case, most topics usually need to be narrowed considerably before they can generate researchable questions (Labovitz & Hagedorn 1971, Kane 1984, Lewis & Munn 1997). Booth et al. (2003) suggest that topics that cannot be summarized in four or five words are too broad and need further refinement before attempts at formulating research questions are made.

Moving from topics to aims and objectives can be a useful step towards formulating research questions. Aims and objectives provide more direction than do topics and can help you start thinking about exactly what you want to achieve in your study. While the aims and objectives of a study tend to be less specific than research questions they are more useful than topics or areas of interest for directing an investigation. Unlike topics, they identify the outcomes (or 'goals') that are desired and point to the kind of questions that would need to be asked in order to achieve these outcomes. The *directive* role played by aims, objectives and purposes can be very valuable, and thinking about the goals of a research project can be a useful intermediary stage between deciding on a topic and formulating research questions.

An example of an objective and some corresponding research questions is provided below:

OBJECTIVE

To find out why certain individuals and groups adopt new technologies before others.

RESEARCH QUESTIONS

1. What are the patterns of consumption of new technologies amongst different groups of adults in the United Kingdom?
2. What reasons do different individuals provide for adopting or not adopting new technologies?

As you can see, it is often necessary to break down a single objective into more than one question. Indeed, this particular objective could have been broken down into three or even four questions. It is also important to notice that the language in the research questions is much more specific than in the objective. The study has been limited to researching adults residing in the United Kingdom, for example. It would also be necessary to provide a working definition of 'new technologies' before any data could be collected. The language used in research questions is a topic that is returned to later. The important point in terms of the present discussion is that reformulating your aims or objectives as research questions forces you to think more carefully about what you want to find out and can help you be more specific about what you want to achieve in your study.

As is the case with topics or areas, the more clearly defined the aims the better they are able to direct your research (Denscombe 2002).

Vague aims and objectives can lead to researchers being over-ambitious, collecting unnecessary data, floundering in too much data and wasting their time down 'blind alleys'. This is also true for poorly formulated research questions, of course. While it is possible for aims and objectives to be stated sufficiently precisely to guide an investigation (in which case it would be a fairly simple matter to derive research questions from them), it is often more helpful to think about your research in terms of the questions you want to answer.

Key Points

- Topics and areas of interest are useful starting points for a study
- Thinking about the aims and objectives of your research can also be a useful exercise
- Reformulating your aims and objectives as research questions will force you to think more carefully about what you want to find out
- The more specific your objectives or research questions, the easier it will be to design and plan your data collection and analysis

---

THE FORM OF QUESTIONS AND THEIR CONTENT

Not all questions are social science research questions. Some questions do not relate to the social world and so are beyond the scope of social research. Other questions might be interesting to social scientists but cannot be answered using empirical evidence and so are not 'researchable'. In this section, some common problems with the form and content of research questions are highlighted to help new researchers avoid formulating problematic questions.

Problems of form

Problems of form relate to the way a question is *structured* rather than the *subject matter* it addresses. Three problems relating to the form of questions are examined below, alongside advice on how they can be avoided.

Questions and other statements

Questions should always be 'open-ended'. If a sentence cannot properly be followed by a question mark, it is not an interrogative statement, and it cannot be considered to be a question. Questions invite a direct response and so are 'open' in a way that other statements are not. Posing a question suggests that a dialogue is unfinished and that the questioner seeks additional information (Fischer 1970).

Some readers may think that this point is so obvious that it does not need stating. It is akin to pointing out that 'questions should be questions'. However, when asked to state their research questions, it is common even for experienced researchers to reply with declarative statements rather than questions (Punch 1998). In my experience, for example, undergraduate and postgraduate students often reply that they want to 'prove' a particular relationship or 'demonstrate' the existence of a particular phenomenon or effect.

The situation is complicated a little because of the relationship between research questions and hypotheses. Both are useful in empirical inquiry but while research questions are interrogative, hypotheses are declarative statements. These statements, however, are intended to be tested (not *proven*) and, as is discussed later in this chapter, play a particular role in scientific inquiry. As hypotheses can easily be reformulated as questions, the two are in some ways 'two sides of the same coin'.

A theme that runs throughout this book is that it is important, for many reasons, to begin an investigation with a question or set of questions. While we all use questions in our daily lives and can easily distinguish them from other statements, it is not always so straightforward to translate ideas for a research project into a set of questions. This is, however, one of the most important stages of the research process. It is vital that investigators translate their ideas into question form as soon as it is possible. First versions of a research question may need considerable modification, and questions may change over the course of a study, but moving on to construct a research design should only be attempted *after* a set of questions have initially been generated.

'Many questions' and 'false dichotomies'

Methods texts often caution against asking respondents two questions at once, usually in the context of conducting interviews or questionnaires. However, it is also unhelpful for research questions to include more than one question, for a number of reasons.

Including more than one inquiry in a single question has been called 'the fallacy of many questions'. This fallacy can arise in several ways, some of which are more obvious than others. Fischer (1970, p. 8) identifies four ways this problem can arise:

1. Framing a question in such a way that two or more questions are asked at once, and a single answer is required.
2. Framing a question in such a way as to beg another question.
3. Framing a question which makes a false presumption.
4. Framing a complex question but demanding a simple answer.

The first type of question is easy to avoid. Although many commentators warn against having too many research questions (see Chapter 3) a sentence that contains more than one question can usually be split unproblematically into two single questions. For example, 'What were the aims of comprehensivisation and to what extent were these aims achieved?' is a compound question; it actually contains two separate questions. Indeed, it requires two separate, albeit related, answers in order to be addressed satisfactorily. This question could easily be separated into the following:

1. What were the aims of comprehensivization?
2. To what extent were these aims achieved?

It is important to separate these elements because each of the two questions has different implications for the kind of data collection and analysis that would be required to address it. The question 'What were the aims of comprehensivisation?' may require the retrieval and analysis of policy documents, and perhaps also interviews with policy-makers and other key stakeholders involved in the process. 'To what extent were these aims achieved?' is a question that can only be asked after the aims of comprehensivization have first been established. It may require, for example, an analysis of secondary data on educational attainment and perhaps also the use of interviews to gain an insight into the experiences of students. While the relationship between research questions and research design is explored in greater depth in Chapter 4, the importance of research questions in directing the collection and analysis of data cannot be overstated. Well-formulated research questions should indicate exactly what data are required to answer them satisfactorily and what type of research design is needed to generate such data. As the example above illustrates, separating compound questions into their component parts is helpful simply because it differentiates between individual elements of an inquiry. This, in turns, leads to clearer thinking about what data are required and how they should best be collected and analysed.

There are other, less obvious ways in which a single question can require more than one answer. The second and third of Fischer's (1970) 'many question' types are those questions that 'beg' another question, or require an additional question to be answered before they can be addressed, and those that make false presumptions.

The following is an example of a question that appears at first sight to contain only one question but makes a false presumption:

At what age do boys stop underachieving at school?

The problem with this question is that it makes two presumptions: not only that boys *do* underachieve at some stage in their educational careers but also that this underachievement disappears at a later point. Both these facts need to be established before such a question can be asked. Assuming that a suitable definition of underachievement has been provided (see Smith 2005 for problems with this) it is possible to improve on this question by asking

1. Do boys 'underachieve' at any point in their compulsory schooling?
2. If so, during which periods of their schooling do they 'underachieve'?

These questions are far from perfect and, given that there tends to be variation within any social group, these questions might be further refined as follows:

1. Do boys 'underachieve' at any time during the compulsory schooling?
2. If so, which type of boys tend to 'underachieve'?
3. What is the timing and duration of any 'underachievement'?
4. Is the timing and duration of any 'underachievement' related to the characteristics of the 'underachievers'?

These questions are still some way from being fully developed but this example demonstrates the kind of processes that are involved in reformulating research questions in order to clarify the elements of an investigation. The original question contained certain assumptions and could only be meaningfully asked if these assumptions were warranted. In order to establish whether these assumptions had any basis in fact, it was first necessary to pose some additional, preliminary, questions. As this example demonstrates, some questions cannot even be *asked*, let alone answered, without a careful consideration of the assumptions that underlie them. *Descriptive* questions usually have to be answered before *explanatory* ones can be addressed, an issue that is returned to later in this chapter.

Problems with research questions often originate in a failure to consider all the stages of inquiry that must be undertaken before certain questions can even be raised. Thinking through these stages can lead both to better research questions and, as a consequence, a greater awareness of the data that are required to address them.

A particular form of the 'fallacy of many questions' is the 'false dichotomous' question. Fischer (1970, pp. 9–10) warns against using this question type, as to do so properly is very difficult. This is because a dichotomy is a division into two parts, and if 'properly drawn, the parts are mutually exclusive and collectively exhaustive, so that there is no overlap, no opening in the middle, and nothing omitted at either end'. If these conditions are not met in full, a dichotomy is used incorrectly. Carrying on the theme of one of the previous questions, an incorrectly formulated dichotomous question reads as follows:

Comprehensive education: force for equality or lowest common denominator?

While this may be fine as an essay question, where the purpose is to stimulate debate, it is not a good research question. It assumes that comprehensive education is *either* a 'force for equality' *or* 'lowest common denominator' and that there is no middle ground between the two. It also assumes that these two situations cannot co-exist. Given the hotly contested definition of 'equality' (see Williams 1989) this would be a very controversial assumption to make.

An additional problem with dichotomous questions is that the term 'or' can be confusing. As Fischer (1970, p. 11) points out, 'or' can mean

a) either X or Y but not both
b) either X or Y or both
c) either X or Y or both, or neither

In essay questions, this kind of ambiguity is fine, as it leaves all three possibilities open and can encourage discussion. But research questions should be as clear and precise as possible, leaving little scope for alternative readings or misinterpretations. Because of this, it is advisable to avoid using the term 'or' in your research questions, unless its inclusion is *absolutely* necessary.

Tautological questions

Tautological questions are problematic because they are both true by definition and because they ask the same question twice. An example of a tautological research question might be

Why are the working classes over-represented in some types of occupation?

At first sight this may appear to be a perfectly reasonable question for a social scientist to ask. To start with, it is a genuinely open question. If we assume, for the sake of argument, that it has already been established that the working class are over-represented in certain types of occupation, then the question avoids making any false presumptions. So why is this question problematic?

The difficulty with this question is that the type of work a person is employed in is central to most definitions of social or occupational class. People are defined as working class at least partly *because* of the kind of occupations in which they are employed. This question is therefore redundant as it already supplies the answer: the working class are over-represented in certain types of occupation because working in these occupations leads people to be defined as working class.

There are a number of ways that this question could be reframed, the form and content of which will depend upon exactly what stimulates the researcher's curiosity. It may be for example, that they are interested in inter-generational mobility and wish to examine barriers to social mobility over time. In this case an appropriate question might be something like

What factors keep children from working-class backgrounds employed in working-class jobs for most of their lives?

Of course, to avoid making a false presumption (see above) it is first necessary to establish that at least some children from working-class backgrounds *are* employed in working-class jobs for most of their lives. But the point here is that, in contrast to the earlier example, this question is not tautological. It is neither self-evidently true, nor does it ask the same question twice.

Key Points

- Avoid using compound questions at all times
- Problems with compound questions can usually be resolved by breaking them down into their constituent parts
- Check that your research questions do not contain false presumptions
- Avoid using the term 'or' in your research questions if at all possible
- Do not ask research questions that are tautological

Problems of subject

As well as being appropriately structured, it is important that your research questions address topics suitable for social scientific investigation. Some questions cannot be answered using empirical evidence and so should be avoided altogether. Metaphysical, ethical and aesthetic questions, for example, all fall outside the realm of social science. In the following sections, some common problems with the subject of research questions are examined, starting with the issue of metaphysical questions.

Metaphysical questions

Metaphysical questions relate to debates that cannot be resolved through empirical inquiry (Cozby et al. 1989). Such questions inquire into the nature of existence, mind, matter, space and time, and, as Fischer (1970, p. 12) argues, 'will not be resolved before the oceans freeze over'.

Whilst it is unlikely that a social scientist would ask an obviously metaphysical question such as 'Do numbers exist independently of human thought?', there are more subtle ways in which metaphysical elements can creep into research questions. Fischer (1970) argues that 'why' questions tend to be metaphysical because the term is difficult to define, and lacks direction and clarity. 'Why' questions, he argues, are not consistent in terms of the type of answer that is required. They can seek causes, motives, reasons, descriptions, processes, purposes or justifications. Because of this, he argues that the other five W-Questions ('who', 'what', 'when', 'where' and 'how' – see below) are much more practical and should be used in place of 'why' whenever possible.

While Fischer's (1970) objection to the term 'why' may, at first sight, appear to be mere hair-splitting, it is simply a call for greater clarity and precision when formulating questions. The problem with this term lies in its ambiguity. The other five W-Questions are, arguably, more precise and their meanings are less subject to variation. Avoiding the use of 'why' may actually lead to better, more clearly specified research questions. Attempting to rephrase 'why' questions would certainly be a good exercise, as it focuses attention on the essence of an inquiry and, as a consequence, the kind of data that would be required.

Similar, but perhaps weaker, objections could be made regarding the use of the term 'how'. While less problematic than 'why', this term still leaves room for some ambiguity. It has even been suggested that all the W-Questions can be reformulated unproblematically as 'what' questions (Hamblin 1967). 'When', for example, can be reformulated as 'at what time', and 'where' can be rephrased as 'at what place'. Similar results can be obtained with 'who', 'why' and 'how'.

Normative questions

Normative questions relate to judgements concerning value or virtue. They are often concerned with what 'ought to be' or 'should be', what is 'desirable' or 'undesirable', what is 'right' and 'wrong', or what is 'good' or 'bad'. In philosophy, normative statements are contrasted with 'descriptive' statements, which can in principle be tested through observation. Normative questions are often concerned with ethical or aesthetic judgements. Such questions have also been called 'deliberative questions' (Dillon 1984).

A simple example of a normative question is

> *Should corporal punishment be re-introduced in secondary schools?*

The main problem with this question is the inclusion of the term 'should'. This is not a question about the effect that corporal punishment has on a particular facet of students' schooling, rather it is a question seeking an opinion about an ethical issue. It cannot be resolved empirically because there is no one correct answer. While moral and ethical questions often contain words such as 'should', 'ought' or 'better than', these are best avoided in social scientific research questions and hypotheses as they tend to invite the expression of opinion rather than recourse to empirical evidence (Nachmias & Nachmias 1976, Kerlinger 1986, Andrews 2002).

It should be noted that although normative questions cannot be resolved through empirical investigation, normative views can be the *subject* of such inquiry. A research question relating to the topic above might read

What proportion of parents think corporal punishment should be re-introduced in secondary schools?

This question clearly has a single, correct answer and it could certainly be addressed by a well-designed and competently executed research project. But, unlike the previous questions it does not chase a definitive moral judgement; alternatively it seeks to determine the weight of opinion on this matter among a clearly defined population of interest.

The following, more subtle, normative question is adapted from an example provided by Kerlinger (1986, p. 21):

Does authoritarian teaching lead to poor learning?

While this question contains none of the 'give-away' terms often found in normative questions, such as 'should' or 'ought', two of the terms used are problematic. The term 'poor' is both vague and suggests a value judgement. It is impossible to determine what is meant by 'poor learning', as this depends on what type of learning is valued by whoever posed the question. Replacing these terms with 'effective learning' may appear to be less problematic but can also cause problems if not linked to clearly defined outcomes (see later discussion).

'Learning' is another term that is too vague to be useful in a research question but it is 'authoritarian' that most obviously invites a value judgement. Although there is a degree of consensus about what 'authoritarian' means, whether or not a particular situation or teaching method would be classified as such depends upon individual preferences and perceptions. A teaching method cannot simply be characterized as 'authoritarian' or 'not authoritarian'; the same situation may be given either label depending on who is doing the labelling. This decision will depend ultimately on how desirable certain aspects of teaching practice, such as rigorously enforced discipline, are to those making the judgement.

It is sometimes easy to identify a normative question by the inclusion of terms such as 'should', 'ought' and 'better'. However, as Kerlinger's (1986) example demonstrates, value-laden terms might not always be immediately obvious. The only foolproof way to guard against this problem is to scrutinize every term in a question and attempt to define them. You need to be particularly careful about words that might appear to be universally understood, such as 'successful', 'effective', 'satisfaction', 'frequent' and 'elderly' (Kane 1984). While these terms may not appear to be problematic at first sight, they are value laden, will vary according to context, and need to be defined and operationalized very carefully if they are to be used at all (see Chapter 4). It is probably best to avoid such terms altogether, unless they are absolutely central to an investigation.

Data collection questions

It is very important to differentiate between research questions and data collection questions (DCQs) (Mason 1996, Punch 1998). Research questions are the questions that the research is designed to address and that guide the conduct of the project. DCQs are questions that are posed during data collection, in a questionnaire or interview for example. The two types of questions serve different purposes.

Gorard (2003a) warns that a common mistake in questionnaire design is to ask respondents the research question rather than a DCQ. I have experienced this a number of times when agreeing to participate in a research project, as the following example illustrates. A questionnaire I received from a doctoral student who was researching the working conditions of academic staff in UK universities included questions of the following type:

1. Do the lecturing staff in your institution feel they are over-worked?
2. Do the lecturing staff in your institution think they are under-paid?

The main problem with these questions stems from the fact that they are only slightly modified versions of the study's research questions. The researcher was clearly interested in the degree to which academic staff felt they were over-worked and/or over-paid. However, instead of asking individuals to report their views on their own situations and then collating the results, he made the mistake of asking them about the general situation in their institution. The problem with this approach is that while individuals may be perfectly able to provide information relating to their own pay and conditions and report their perceptions of these, they are unlikely to have access to the views of all the other members of staff in their institutions. Indeed, they would need to have conducted a research project themselves in order to obtain this information. Furthermore, even if they did so, they still would have not been able to answer the question satisfactorily, because it would be extremely unlikely that all the responses would have been the same. The likely result would have been that a certain proportion of staff thought they were over-worked, for example, and a certain proportion thought otherwise.

A more appropriate way of formulating these DCQs would be as follows:

1. Do you think you are over-worked?
2. Do you think you are under-paid?

The responses to these questions could then have been collated, enabling the researcher to ascertain the proportion of staff who believed they were over-worked, and the proportion reporting that they were under-paid.

When formulating research questions, it is important that they take an appropriate form, and are not confused with DCQs. It is less common, in my experience, for novice researchers to present DCQs as research questions, but students often find it difficult to distinguish between the two. The main point to remember is that it is rarely, if ever, appropriate to ask respondents the research questions directly. It is almost always the case that DCQs must take a different form from the research questions.

Key Points

- Any research questions you formulate must be answerable using empirical evidence
- 'Why' questions can lack direction and clarity, and may be better formulated using one of the other 'W-Questions'
- Questions relating to value judgements should always be avoided
- It is important not to confuse your research questions with your data collection questions

QUESTION TYPES

> The kinds of question we ask are as many as the kinds of things
> which we know.
>
> Aristotle (Posterior Analytics) (89b)

In the first part of this chapter, it has been argued that there are
different kinds of questions, some that can be answered by social
research and some that cannot. There is, however, considerable
variation even amongst those questions that we have decided are
social scientific research questions. But how do they differ? And
what are the most important differences?

In order to answer these questions, some authors have developed
'typologies' of research questions. Examining your research
questions in terms of these typologies can be very useful, as this
process can help you think about what kind of questions you are
asking and, consequently, the type of data you will need in order
to answer them. Some of the most useful typologies are examined
directly below, alongside advice about how they can help you clarify the goals of your research.

Descriptive and explanatory questions

One of the most useful typologies is provided by de Vaus (2001,
p. 1) who divides research questions into two categories, 'descriptive'
and 'explanatory'. He argues that social researchers pose two
fundamental types of research questions:

1. *What* is going on? (descriptive research)
2. *Why* is it going on? (explanatory research)

It is useful to distinguish between these types of questions for
several reasons. Firstly, as was noted earlier in this chapter, it is
important to recognize that descriptive questions usually precede
explanatory ones, as 'before asking "Why?" we must be sure about
the fact and dimensions of the phenomenon' (de Vaus 2001, p. 2).
Because of this, dividing questions into these types can help you
decide which much be tackled first and which can be left until later.
And as different kinds of data are needed to answer descriptive and

explanatory questions, dividing them in this way will help you plan your research design (see Chapter 4).

Dividing questions into descriptive and explanatory types is certainly a useful first step. However, as discussed in the previous section, 'Why?' questions are sometimes problematic because they do not indicate precisely the kind of data they require. Reformulating your 'Why?' questions using any of the other five W-Question types (see below) may make it easier to pinpoint exactly what data you need to collect.

W-Questions: four descriptive and two explanatory question types

The W-Questions or Journalistic Six – 'who', 'what', 'where', 'when', 'why' and 'how' – are often used by journalists as an 'imaginative checklist' to generate questions relating to a particular topic or incident. They are also used in many other areas, such as creative writing and business planning, to stimulate innovative thinking. Their strength lies in their familiarity, and they are certainly a good place to start when generating initial ideas for research questions.

The W-Questions can be usefully divided to correspond with de Vaus's (2001) typology, as shown in Table 2.1.

Thinking about your research in terms of the W-Questions can be useful if you have decided on a topic or area of interest but have yet to formulate any specific research questions. Attempting to rewrite your ideas as sentences that include these terms will help you move from statements about what you want your research to achieve to direct questions that you intend to address. You should then

Table 2.1 Descriptive and explanatory questions

Descriptive Questions	Explanatory Questions
What	How
Who	Why
When	
Where	

be able to divide your questions into those that are 'descriptive' in their aims and those that are 'explanatory'. This can help you structure and prioritize your questions so that you can turn your attention to the kind of data you will require.

Purpose-led typologies

Whether you have reached the stage of formulating research questions or not, it can be useful to think about the *purpose* of your research. As mentioned previously, being clear about the purpose of your study is no substitute for a set of research questions but thinking about what you intend to achieve in your research may help you focus your ideas.

Even if you *have* formulated a set of research questions, thinking about the purpose of individual questions can be a useful exercise. Considering the purpose of a question can help clarify the role that it plays in the wider context of a study and even suggest whether it is a necessary element of a particular investigation. As is discussed in the next chapter, it is sometimes necessary to reduce an initial list of questions into a smaller more tightly focused set. Thinking about the purpose of every question, and the relationship between them, can help you with this task. And as with almost every activity that requires you to think carefully about the questions you are asking, thinking about the purpose of your questions will also naturally lead to a consideration of data collection and analysis.

Denscombe (2002, p. 26) divides questions into six types, according to purpose:

1. Forecasting an outcome or making predictions
2. Explaining causes or consequences
3. Criticizing or evaluating
4. Description
5. Developing good practice
6. Empowerment

I have provided the following examples to illustrate questions that correspond to the different purposes outlined by Denscombe.

While some of the questions are quite similar, they are all phrased in slightly different ways in order to reflect their underlying purpose:

1. What do current trends suggest about future levels of membership in political parties in the United Kingdom?
2. What factors are associated with membership of political parties in the United Kingdom?
3. To what extent have recent initiatives impacted on the level of membership in political parties in the United Kingdom?
4. How did patterns of political-party membership change in the United Kingdom between 1979 and 2007?
5. What administrative measures are most effective in reducing rates of unplanned lapses in party membership?

Categorizing your research questions according to this typology can help you clarify exactly what each question aims to achieve and how your questions fit together to fulfil the overall aim of the study. This may help you order your research questions, either into a sequence or hierarchy, or reveal that some of your questions do not fit well with the others. In such cases, do not be too cautious about discarding some of your original questions. It is better to have a less ambitious, more tightly focused study than one that is incoherent and vague.

'Empowerment'

I feel that a note of caution should be sounded in relation to Denscombe's category, 'empowerment'. While many researchers are concerned with empowering particular individuals or groups through the conduct of research, the clearest route to this objective is through the conduct of high-quality empirical research. The first step to help-ing a disadvantaged group is the provision of accurate information about the nature and extent of their disadvantage, and the context in which it arises and is sustained. All too often, the political motives of researchers can interfere with the research process and jeopardize the integrity and rigor of a study. This can lead to the paradoxical situ-ation where those researchers who are most vocal about the needs of a disadvantaged or minority group can impede effective policy or practice interventions because of the questionable nature of the evidence base they have produced. Hammersley (1999) provides a useful discussion of the dangers of politically motivated research.

Agendas of 'empowerment' are, in short, best avoided in social research. A researcher who endeavours to describe and explain the circumstances of a disadvantaged group can, however, produce knowledge that may be used by policy-makers and practitioners to implement ameliorative measures aimed at improving the situation of that group. Understanding the social world is a necessary precursor to improving it.

Comparison

An important term that is missing from both de Vaus's (2001) and Denscombe's (2002) typologies is 'comparison'. Making appropriate comparisons is an essential part of social research but one that can easily be overlooked (Gorard 2003a). Dillon (1984) suggests that comparison usually takes place *after* descriptive questions have been addressed but *before* explanations have been sought. A very simple, yet comprehensive, model of the research process might be as follows:

1. Description
2. Comparison
3. Explanation

While it can be argued that comparison is part of the descriptive stage of research, I feel it deserves a separate category simply to remind students and new researchers of its importance. I regularly read reports of research that is fatally flawed because of the author's failure to make appropriate comparisons. These problems are not only common in research conducted by undergraduate students but can also be found in articles published in high ranking peer-reviewed academic journals. This suggests that comparison is frequently overlooked by both those responsible for conducting research and those responsible for ensuring its quality.

It is fairly common for researchers to pay insufficient attention to this sequence of inquiry. Many studies have devoted considerable time and resources attempting to explain phenomena that have not been adequately established though careful description. During the 1990s and early 2000s, for example, researchers went to great lengths to explain why a shortage of teachers had reached crisis proportions and was steadily worsening. Pay levels, morale, workload and student discipline were commonly cited as 'explanations' for this crisis, and policy initiatives followed in the form of financial incentives to train, performance-related pay and media recruitment campaigns. A careful examination of existing data sets, however, revealed that there were more teachers than ever, in a context of declining student numbers, with nearly twice as many applicants as available places in training courses (see Gorard et al. (2006a) for a detailed report). Most researchers had been so keen to look for explanations for this apparent 'crisis' that they over-looked the task of carefully describing the very situation they were attempting to explain.

As the example above illustrates, while the prospect of *explaining* a particular aspect of social life is a very exciting one, it is first necessary to ensure that it has been depicted accurately. It is all too easy to ignore this crucial first step in an inquiry but to do so can jeopardize an entire study. This can have consequences outside of the research community and, as was the case with this example, public money can be wasted trying to solve problems that never really existed.

Categorizing your questions according to their purpose and proper place within the sequence of inquiry can help you avoid making these kinds of mistakes. It will alert you to any descriptive work that needs to be carried out before you attempt to explain a particular phenomenon and will provide guidance as to the different kinds of data that will have to be collected in order to satisfactorily address your research questions.

Key Points

- Typologies can help you think about exactly what type of questions you are asking
- Reformulating your aims and objectives as W-Questions can help you move from topics to questions
- Remember that descriptive questions will need to be answered before explanatory ones can be asked
- Make sure you think about any appropriate comparisons that need to be made

---

HYPOTHESES

Hypotheses are often a source of much confusion amongst students and new researchers. This is not at all surprising, given the strange place that they occupy in the methods literature. They are discussed in great detail in some methods text but are completely ignored in others, and are much more likely to be discussed in texts written between the 1950s and 1970s than in more recent publications. Greater emphasis is paid to testing hypotheses in certain disciplines, such as psychology, than in the social sciences more widely. Hypotheses tend to be associated with 'quantitative' research and statistical analysis but their use is by no means, and *should not* be, restricted to these contexts. And while some authors insist that hypotheses are only useful when derived from existing theory, others suggest that the source of hypotheses is unimportant.

The aim of this section is to clarify the role of hypotheses in social research and, in doing so, to minimize confusion in this area. Hypotheses can be a very useful tool for the researcher but in order for them to be useful it is necessary to understand exactly what they are and how they can be used.

What are hypotheses?

The most important defining characteristic of a hypothesis is that it is a *prediction*. A hypothesis is 'an imaginative preconception of *what might be true*' (Medawar 1972, p. 26). Hypotheses are different from research questions because rather than simply *asking* a question they suggest an *answer* to one. These answers are speculative, however, and need to be tested against empirical evidence before they can be either confirmed or refuted.

Hypotheses and research questions are closely related, however. While the research questions states 'what we are trying to find out', the hypothesis 'predicts ... the answer to that question' (Punch 1998, p. 39). Because a hypothesis is simply a predicted answer to a research question it is important to be clear about the question you are asking as well as the answer you expect. As the following example shows, however, it is usually relatively simple to work backwards from a hypothesis to a research question.

HYPOTHESIS

On average, working mothers spend more time doing housework than employed fathers living in the same household.

RESEARCH QUESTION

Do working mothers spend more time doing housework, on average, than employed fathers living in the same household?

Some authors (e.g. Nachmias & Nachmias 1976) include references to 'dependent' and 'independent' variables, and the relationships between them, in their definitions of hypotheses. Thinking about your research question in terms of variables and relationships can be very useful when planning your research design but is not strictly necessary when you are still generating ideas for research. In the very early stages of your study, it is much more important to be clear what questions you want to address and, in the case of hypotheses, what you expect to find out. If thinking about variables helps you clarify your research questions then it is clearly a useful exercise. However, if this line of thought confuses you, it can safely be left until later in the research process.

Hypotheses are also discussed alongside statistical analysis. Particular types of statistical tests require researchers to formulate two types of hypotheses, 'null' hypotheses and 'alternative' hypotheses. 'Alternative' hypotheses, contrary to what the name suggests, usually state what the researcher has predicted will occur. 'Null' hypotheses, on the other hand, state that this will not be the case. Strictly speaking, researchers should specify their alternative and null hypotheses before conducting inferential statistical tests.

The fact that hypothesis testing is central to some statistical analyses *does not* mean that formulating hypotheses should be *restricted* to this context. As is repeatedly argued in this chapter, hypotheses can be useful in a very wide variety of research designs and their formulation has no necessary link with the kind of analysis conducted. As Punch (1998, p. 41) makes clear, 'there is no logical difference between research questions and research hypotheses, when it comes to their implications for design, data collection and data analysis'.

Neither is it the case, as some commentators have suggested, that hypotheses are only useful if they are derived from theory. This is an unnecessary restriction with no logical basis. Hypotheses can arise in many contexts and, like research questions, are tools to be used by social researchers. After all, they are merely 'hunches' about what you might find out (Verma & Beard 1981).

Hypotheses can be useful because they are often more focused and precise than research questions (Kerlinger 1986). Questions can be asked without any prior knowledge of a topic but some background knowledge is often required in order to generate a hypothesis (Andrews 2003). Hypotheses tend to offer more direction than research questions in terms of both the type of data that need to be collected in a study and also to the way these data must be subsequently analysed (Sellitz et al. 1965, Medawar 1979).

Whether you use hypotheses in your research will depend on many factors, including what you want to find out and whether you have any ideas about what you might find. Hypotheses will be more or less useful in different contexts and there seems little to be gained by insisting that researchers *always* formulate hypotheses at the beginning of a research project. Studies that include hypotheses are not necessarily more scientific than those that do not (Sellitz et al. 1965) and failing to formulate a hypothesis is not necessarily a 'sin of omission', as in some cases hypotheses will simply not arise (Black 1993, p. 31). There is certainly no point in having hypotheses for their own sake, and researchers should not be concerned if their research is led by questions rather than predictions (Punch 1998). The best course of action is to formulate hypotheses when they are useful and appropriate but not to be concerned if you begin your research with only questions rather than predictions about the probable findings of your study.

Key Points

- Hypotheses are *predicted answers* to research questions
- They can help provide focus and direction to your study
- Their use is not restricted to particular types of inquiry
- Don't feel that you *must* formulate a hypothesis – only use them if they are useful

---

Where do hypotheses come from?

Many research projects begin with hypotheses of some kind, even if these are not stated explicitly. Any predictions about the findings of a study are hypothetical, and researchers often have some ideas about what their research might reveal, whether this originates from their previous experience, from reviewing the related literature or is merely an intuitive hunch. Hypotheses are 'tentative answers to research problems' (Nachmias & Nachmias 1976, p. 23) and it is common for researchers to start a study with *some* ideas about the nature of the phenomena they are studying, and the relationships between them (Bulmer 1979).

While the formulation and testing of hypotheses is central to what Punch (1998, p. 26) characterizes as 'theory verification research' (see Chapter 1), the generation of hypotheses is certainly not restricted to this type of inquiry. While theories can provide plenty of opportunities for hypothesis generation, hypotheses frequently arise outside of this context (Sellitz et al. 1965, Robson 1993). Indeed, Medawar (1979, p. 84), a distinguished natural scientist, argues that hypotheses arise 'by a process as easy or as difficult to understand as any other creative act of mind; it is a brainwave, an inspired guess, the product of a blaze of insight. [They come] ... from within and cannot be arrived at by the exercise of any known calculus of discovery'.

Hypotheses and research design

As has already been noted, hypotheses, like research questions, can be useful in providing guidance as to the most appropriate research design for a particular study. It was also argued that hypotheses are more likely to be used in certain types of study, such as those that seek to test well-developed theories. Hypotheses also play a central role in experimental studies and when inferential statistical analyses are necessary.

However, the use of hypotheses should not be restricted to certain research designs. While it has been suggested that their use is only appropriate for 'quantitative empirical research' (see Dillon 1983), and incompatible with 'qualitative studies' (Creswell 2003) and ethnographic research (Dobbert 1982), there are no strong arguments why this is the case and many prominent researchers disagree.

Bell (1993), Guba and Lincoln (1994) and Holliday (2002) all argue that hypotheses can be useful in 'qualitative' research, while Barton and Lazarfield (1969), Spradley (1980) and Reason (1994) view hypothesis testing as perfectly compatible with ethnographic studies. Hammersley and Atkinson (1995, p. 19) write explicitly about the identification and testing of 'hypothetical patterns' and Hymes (1978, in Spradley 1980, p. 31) argues for a 'hypothesis-oriented' ethnography.

Holliday (2002) provides a very useful review of the arguments for and against the use of hypotheses in 'qualitative' research. She concludes that

> hypotheses are used in qualitative research which investigates a relationship between several entities. This essential nature of hypotheses does not have to be restricted to the controlled world of quantitative research. In qualitative research too there can be relationships which the research sets out to investigate in a systematic, though not quantifiable way.
>
> Holliday (2002, p. 34)

The key point in Holliday's (2002) argument is that hypotheses are concerned with the relationship between variables. As most research is concerned with such relationships, there seems little reason to restrict the use of hypotheses to a narrow range of methods of data collection and analysis. Hypotheses may be useful wherever relationships between variables are examined; that is to say, in most social scientific research.

Key Points

- Hypotheses have traditionally been linked to theory testing but any prediction about research findings is 'hypothetical'.
- They can be useful in many different types of study and are not just restricted to 'quantitative' research or statistical analysis.
- Hypotheses are also used by those conducting 'qualitative' and ethnographic research.

SUMMARY

A central aim of this chapter is to show how research questions differ from aims, objectives and other statements about the purpose of your study. It has provided guidance on how to move from a topic or area of interest to a set of research questions that reflect the goals of your research. The problems that can arise with the form and content of questions have also been discussed, as have the different types of questions that you can ask. The final section considered the role of hypotheses in social research and their relationship to research questions.

The next chapter examines the process of turning research questions into *researchable* questions. It outlines the differences between questions that are researchable 'in principle' and those that are researchable 'in practice' and suggests practical strategies for identifying and reformulating unresearchable questions. The central role played by the resources available to the researcher is stressed, and guidance on prioritizing and structuring research questions is offered.

FURTHER READING

A philosophical discussion of the nature of questions can be found in

Hamblin, C.L. (1967) 'Questions', in Edwards, P. (Ed.) *The Encyclopedia of Philosophy: Volume 7*. New York: Macmillan & The Free Press. pp. 49–53.

The most comprehensive review of typologies of research question can be found in Dillon's paper:

Dillon, J.T. (1984) 'The Classification of Research Questions', *Review of Educational Research*, 54 (3), pp. 327–61.

Fischer provides a very comprehensive review of the problems that are encountered when framing research questions.

Fischer, D.H. (1971) *Historians' Fallacies: Toward a Logic of Historical Thought*. London: Routledge and Kegan Paul. ch. 1.

The role of hypotheses in social science is discussed in greater depth in the following texts:

Black, T.R. (1993) *Evaluating Social Science Research: An Introduction*. London: Sage. pp. 28–38.

Kerlinger, F.N. (1986) *Foundations of Behavioural Research*, (3rd Edn.) New York: CBS Publishing.

3 What makes a question 'researchable'?

There are grand ideas, good ideas, and doable ideas…In the case of executing a research project, being able to recognise these differences is essential.

Bradley (2001, p. 569)

In the previous chapter, the nature of questions was examined in some detail. Particular attention was paid to highlighting the problems that can arise when formulating research questions. One of the most important issues raised was the difference between questions that could be addressed through empirical research and those that could not – between 'researchable' and 'unresearchable' questions.

This chapter explores the issue of 'researchability' in greater depth. While the previous chapter was primarily concerned with whether questions were researchable in *principle*, this chapter examines the *practical* constraints that may limit the kind of questions that you can address. The first section highlights general issues that can arise in relation to the researchability of questions. The remainder of the chapter looks at ways in which questions can be changed in order to better match the limitations imposed by the available resources.

THE 'RESEARCHABILITY' OF QUESTIONS

As was discussed in the previous chapter, some questions, by virtue of their form or content, are unresearchable. They are not *social scientific* questions. Questions that, for whatever reasons, cannot be answered by empirical investigation are unresearchable *in principle*, and of little interest to the social scientist.

There are, however, questions that are undoubtedly researchable in principle but which may not be able to be addressed *in practice* because of constraints relating to time and other resources. These questions will be the focus of much of the discussion in this chapter, alongside advice on how such questions can be modified or reformulated to be better suited to a particular context. The aim is to show how questions that are answerable in principle, but are faced with practical problems, can be identified and transformed into questions that are researchable in practice.

A question of scope

As was noted in Chapter 2, one of the most common mistakes made by novice researchers is to be far too ambitious about what their research can achieve. This over-ambition is usually reflected in the research questions they have formulated or in their stated aims or purpose.

This problem invariably arises from inexperience; the extent to which a researcher over-estimates what they can achieve tends to diminish once they have completed their first few projects. Such reassurances, of course, will be of little comfort if you are just about to start your first research project. The following section explores various strategies for setting the limits of a study through 'bounding' research questions, prioritizing particular questions over others, managing the number of questions you ask and creating structured hierarchies that will help direct the collection and analysis of your data.

It is common for early versions of research questions to require a certain amount of work in order to become researchable (Lewis & Munn 1997). Early formulations of research questions are often too vague or address topics that are too broad (Kane 1984, Kerlinger 1986). In the early stages of a study researchers sometimes find it difficult even to explain what their research is intended to investigate. They either produce a 'short but over-general' or 'long and over-detailed' description of the research but cannot sum it up as one or two central research questions (Mason 1996, p. 10).

Research questions that remain unspecified, or are vague or unclear in some way, can lead to many problems later in the course of an investigation. If they are not specified precisely they will not provide the research with sufficient direction (Black 1993). In addition to not indicating exactly which aspects of the topic should be examined, such questions will fail to indicate the most appropriate sources of data or methods of data collection and analysis (Lewis & Munn 1997). This can lead to over-ambitious aims and expectations, being confronted with too much data to collect and analyse, and wasting time with unnecessary data and lines of investigation (Denscombe 2002).

Prioritizing

One of the easiest ways a researcher can bound the scope of their inquiry is by prioritizing their research questions with a view to reducing their overall number. This also has the advantage of focusing the study more tightly and encouraging the investigator to think carefully about what they are *really* interested in finding out.

Once you have identified an interesting topic, you will be confronted with a large number of questions that you *could* address. Whilst it may be useful to generate a long list of research questions initially (Mason 1996), you must resist the temptation to address too many questions in a single study. This is particularly important if conducting your research as part of an undergraduate or masters degree, as your time and other resources will be extremely limited. While you may initially generate quite a large number of questions, these need to be pared down and prioritized before the research can be taken forward (Jorgenson 1989, Booth et al. 2003). Flick (1998, p. 49) suggests that researchers begin by reducing the variety of initially generated research questions by 'structuring the field under study'. This can be done by identifying aspects of a topic which are considered to be the most important and bringing questions relating to these to the fore. Other elements, and the questions that relate to these, can then be discarded.

There are no hard and fast rules for deciding which questions are most important; this will depend on what you are most interested in finding out. Some commentators (e.g. Campbell et al. 1982) argue that certain substantive areas are simply more important than others, but most authors are much less uncompromising, merely suggesting that researchers should be able to defend their choices in front of a professional audience (Jorgenson 1989). For students, the most important (and perhaps only) audience of any importance will be those who are supervising and examining their research project. In such cases, meeting course requirements and expectations of teaching should always be the highest priority.

Andrews (2003) warns of including research questions 'for interest's sake'. As others (e.g. Gorard 2003a) have noted, this is a common mistake in the design of questionnaires and one that can lead to overly long instruments and the generation of unnecessary data. Starting a project with superfluous research questions, however, can have much more serious consequences, as it can impact on the research design in ways that may be costly in terms of time and other precious resources.

Campbell et al. (1982) caution against asking questions simply because it seems feasible to answer them. They note that some questions are popular because relevant data are easily obtainable but the questions themselves are trivial or unimportant. In contrast, other more pressing issues are not addressed because to do so would be very challenging. Whilst it is important to be sure that the questions you pose are researchable, it is also necessary to be confident that your topic of investigation is worth researching.

Key Points

- Generating lots of questions can be initially useful. But try to prioritize the most important ones and discard the others.
- Don't ask questions 'for interest's sake'. This will complicate your study unnecessarily and stretch your time and other resources.
- Don't ask questions just because you think they will be easy to answer. You should be able to justify why your questions are important.

Creating hierarchies: main and subsidiary questions

Once particular questions have been identified as priorities, other questions can be structured around them. It is often useful to order questions hierarchically into 'main' and 'subsidiary' questions (Denscombe 2002). Subsidiary questions (or 'sub-questions') derive from the main question, and answering them can help to answer the main question (Andrews 2003). Creating a hierarchical relationship between questions by dividing them in this way can avoid the confusion caused by having multiple foci in a single project. Questions may need to be re-ordered, reformulated, discarded, combined or amended in order to create a coherent hierarchy, but spending time on this process usually results in a clearer vision of what issues the research is intended to address (Andrews 2003).

The following example, adapted from my own research (White 2007) demonstrates the difference between main and subsidiary research questions.

MAIN RESEARCH QUESTION

How do young people make educational and career decisions at the end of compulsory schooling?

SUBSIDIARY RESEARCH QUESTIONS

a) What factors do young people consider when making their choices?
b) What sources of information do they use to help their decision-making?
c) Which individuals are influential in shaping their choices?

Andrews (2003) would describe my sub-questions as 'contributory' questions. By this, he means that answering these questions would help me address my main question. My main question is too broad to be answered directly but by combining the answers to my subsidiary questions I was able to answer it satisfactorily. Andrews contrasts these with what he calls 'ancillary' sub-questions. These are questions which do not necessarily help answer the main research question but *follow* from it and can only be addressed *after* the main research question has been answered. For the above example, ancillary sub-questions might be as follows.

MAIN RESEARCH QUESTION

How do young people make educational and career decisions at the end of compulsory schooling?

ANCILLARY SUB-QUESTIONS

a) How do decisions made at this point affect their future career trajectories?
b) Do young people make decisions in similar ways at later points in their educational careers?

The ancillary sub-questions in this example do not help answer the main question. In fact, they broaden the scope of the study by asking questions that, although related to the main question, would require additional data to be collected. In contrast, addressing the *contributory* sub-questions in the first example requires no additional data. Any data needed to address these questions would contribute to answering the main question. In fact, the main question could not be answered satisfactorily *without* these data.

Because ancillary sub-questions tend to broaden the scope of a study, rather than provide focus and direction, they are best avoided in most small-scale research projects. They can often only be addressed *after* the main question has been answered and do not help answer the main question itself. After you have divided your research questions hierarchically, into 'main' and 'subsidiary' questions, it is useful to identify and remove any ancillary questions and to concentrate your efforts on developing the main and contributory questions.

How many research questions?

It is common for students to ask how many research questions their research should address. While there is no 'right' answer to this question, several commentators have provided advice in this area, with recommendations ranging from one or two main questions (Stone 2002, Creswell 2003) to no more than a dozen (Miles & Huberman 1994). For all but the very largest projects, a maximum of four general questions seems to be a good rule of thumb, although the scope of each question must also be taken into consideration (see later discussion). Novice researchers should be wary of being over-ambitious in the early stages of research, and would be advised to restrict themselves to one or two main questions.

You should also aim to keep the number of 'subsidiary' questions manageable. Again, opinions vary on a suitable number but vary between two or three (Punch 1998) and five to seven (Creswell 2003). The small discrepancies between individual views on the number of main and subsidiary questions tends to be in opposite directions, however, meaning that the total number of questions advised by most authors appears to be somewhere between twelve and fourteen.

Students conducting research projects as part of undergraduate or masters degrees should aim to keep the total number of their research questions well below this limit, if at all possible. Unless the subsidiary questions are very simple to answer, addressing more than three or four sub-questions is likely to be difficult with the available time and other resources. Whilst each study will necessarily be different, novice researchers are advised to restrict the total number of research questions to a maximum of six.

Key Points

- Ordering your questions by placing them into hierarchies can help you prioritize some questions over others.
- Dividing questions into 'main' and 'subsidiary' categories can also help you identify which questions are central to your study.
- Questions will often need to be re-ordered, reformulated, combined or discarded before you finish working on them.
- Try to avoid 'ancillary' questions that broaden the scope of your study.

The scope of your research questions can be effectively bounded by prioritizing, structuring and limiting their number. These activities will also serve to clarify the focus of a study and to make the process of research design considerably more straightforward. The language used in each question, however, is also important.

A QUESTION OF LANGUAGE

The language used in research questions has direct implications not only for communicating the purpose of the research but also for the kind of research design that is appropriate for a particular investigation. Because of this, it is vital that research questions are carefully worded. They should be as clear and concise as possible, and capture the essence of the inquiry succinctly and precisely.

The degree to which research questions meet these criteria is usually a good indicator of how thoroughly the ideas behind a study have been thought through. It is unusual for even experienced researchers' first attempts at research questions to be completely satisfactory (Lewis & Munn 1997) and questions will often need to be revised several times (Hudson-Barr 2005). Lewis and Munn (1997, p. 2) advise spending as much time as is needed 'clarifying in advance *what* you need to know and *why* you need to know it'. The difficulty of this task should not be underestimated; it can be even more challenging than actually conducting the research or writing up the findings (Kane 1984) and is a process that can be very time consuming.

It is important that your research questions are as clear, precise and brief as possible. Advice on achieving all three of these characteristics in your questions is provided in the sections below.

Brevity

It is important not only to restrict the number of questions addressed in a single study but also to express each question as concisely as possible. Both Stone (2002) and Kane (1984) suggest that all research questions should be posed as a single sentence, even if this initially appears impossible. Kane (1984, p. 20) warns that 'most people tend to believe that *their* research is too complex to be expressed in a single sentence' but that the very process of attempting to do so is useful for clarifying your aims and focus. She believes that this goal is usually, if not always, achievable and questions that are not brief and succinct are usually indicators of researchers not having thought sufficiently carefully about what they want to achieve.

Reworking initial questions into more concisely expressed forms may be challenging and require considerable effort. This work is by no means wasted, however, as greater attention to such matters at the beginning of the research process pays dividends during the process of planning the data collection and analysis. It must also be considered that it is possible to end up with questions that are *too* brief and do not provide sufficient information. There will always be a compromise between keeping a question brief and including sufficient information to define the limits of the research precisely (see later discussion).

Key Points

- Keep your research questions as brief and concise as possible.
- Research questions should not usually be longer than one sentence. If they are, they are likely to contain more than one question.
- But make sure your questions include important details.

Clarity

Defining key terms is central to achieving clarity in a research question (Nachmias & Nachmias 1976). This is important both for the researcher and the reader, as being unclear about the meaning of concepts can lead to misinterpretations of both research aims *and* findings (Fischer 1970).

Kane (1984, p. 20) recommends examining every word in a research question and, if necessary, defining 'each noun, verb, adjective and adverb'. This process should aim to 'restrict the scope of each word as much as possible without interfering with what you hope to study'. She warns researchers to be particularly careful with terms that many people might assume to have common meanings, such as 'frequent', 'effective', 'successful', 'elderly' and 'satisfaction'. While this may take some time, it should ensure that there is little room for ambiguity in the resulting questions.

It is vital that both you and your readers share the same interpretation of *all* the concepts you use in your research, and that you are clear about the origin of particular definitions and your rationale for their use. This contributes to the overall transparency of the research process and allows the quality of your research to be evaluated. As is discussed in Chapter 4, where the process of operationalizing concepts is explored in detail, some terms will be easier to operationalize than others, and it may sometimes be necessary to make small changes to research questions when particular terms become too problematic. If you are using particularly abstract concepts, it is more likely that you will encounter difficulties at this stage of the research. As Sellitz et al. (1965) argue, 'the greater the distance between one's concepts, or constructs, and the empirical facts to which they are intended to refer, the greater the possibility of their being misunderstood or carelessly used, and the greater care that must be given to defining them'. When it comes to concepts and their definitions, novice researchers are advised to err on the side of simplicity, even if this means narrowing the scope of their research or restricting the generalizability of their findings.

A common problem relating to clarity is identified by Kane (1984, p. 16). She bemoans the tendency of some researchers to 'dress up' a topic to make it more scientific, a practice that she believes reflects 'the idea that research, to be research, must be festooned with impressive "academic"-sounding language'. As is discussed in Chapter 4, this tendency is often combined with the equally problematic use of theoretical constructs that are neither clearly defined nor meaningfully operationalizable. Medawar (1972, p. 29) dismisses the view that some ideas, by virtue of their profundity, cannot be expressed clearly, concluding that 'no one who has something original or important to say will willingly run the risk of being misunderstood; people who write obscurely are either unskilled in writing or up to mischief'.

Research questions should be expressed as simply as possible with technical language kept to an absolute minimum. As a general rule, all jargon should be avoided unless its absence would significantly alter the nature of the investigation. Some technical terms may be necessary for particular inquiries but the essence of *all* research questions should be able to be expressed in everyday language. A useful yardstick for such an exercise might be communicating the aims of your research via a press release. Thinking about how your research questions could be translated into language suitable for transmission in the mainstream media can be a useful 'grounding' exercise that prompts reflection about what your research intends to achieve and why it is worth doing.

Summary

- It is vital that your research questions are as clear and unambiguous as possible
- Think about each word in your research questions and how it could be interpreted
- Avoid unnecessary technical language terms that could easily be mis-interpreted

Precision

In addition to being clear, research questions should also be as precise as possible. Research questions that are too vague or general are relatively common, even amongst professional researchers (see Campbell et al. 1982, Bordage 2001) and as is the case with lack of clarity, this can cause problems for both those conducting the research and those reading it. Research questions that lack precision and specificity often cannot provide enough direction for the research design and lead to poorly designed research (Morrison 2002, Stone 2002). As vague questions tend to produce vague answers, findings from such studies are often inconclusive and of limited use (Black 1993, Denscombe 2002).

Progressing from initial ideas about topics of interest to well-defined research questions can be difficult precisely because it involves moving from the vague to the specific. The following three stage exercise, intended to help ease this transition, is adapted from the work of Booth et al. (2003):

1. Name your topic
This first stage involves describing your topic as precisely as you can. Ideally this should be done in a single sentence. Such a sentence might take the following form:

'*I am trying to learn about* _____ ....'

2. Make your topic more specific
Add a clause to your sentence that provides more focus and makes your inquiry more specific. It might help to include at least one of the Six-W words discussed in Chapter 2. This might be something like

'*...because I want to find out who/what/when/where/whether/ why/how* _____ ...'

3. Motivate your question
The final part of this exercise provides a justification for your study. It should help explain why you are interested in this particular aspect of this topic. It could take a similar form to the clause below:

'*in order to understand* _____'

Following this sequence of questions can help you focus your inquiry. It is only the first step in moving from a topic to a fully formed set of research questions but it is a good place to begin. It is often the case that the most difficult part of this process is actually finding a starting point to work from, and this exercise is intended to provide exactly that. When you are satisfied that you have narrowed the focus of your inquiry sufficiently, the statement of intent you have formulated needs to be translated into a series of questions. Questions can then be ordered and organized according to the guidelines provided earlier in this chapter.

A precisely stated research question needs to include certain information. In particular, it must be explicit about the 'what', the 'who', the 'where' and the 'when' of the research (Stone 2002,

Hudson-Barr 2005). Unless the information is redundant, research questions should always include the answers to the following questions:

a) What is the focus of the project?
b) Who is to be studied?
c) Where is the research to be conducted?
d) When will the research be conducted?

These questions correspond to the following areas of information:

a) The substantive area of interest.
b) The population of interest and, if appropriate, study sample.
c) The study site or region.
d) The historical period covered by the fieldwork or data.

The following example, adapted from Morrison (2002, p. 90) demonstrates how all of this information can be included in a single research question:

> Why do (*why?*) second year (*when*) medical students (*who*) at Glasgow University (*where*) prefer learning about ethics (*what*) in small groups (*how*)?

This is a particular type of research question that depends upon a quite specific existing knowledge base (i.e. that it has already been established, by descriptive research, that these students *do* prefer to learn in small groups). It also contains elements (the 'how' and 'why') that may either be inappropriate or superfluous to some inquires and, as was discussed in Chapter 2, can be problematic. Nevertheless, it illustrates how a great deal of information regarding the details of an inquiry can be incorporated very concisely into a relatively short research question.

The process of constructing clear and precise research questions can help focus your mind on what exactly you wish to achieve in your study. However, having clear ideas about the direction of an inquiry does not automatically lead to the formulation of clear and precise questions. The very fact that *you* are clear about what you intend to find out can lead to the neglect of certain aspects of question formulation simply because this information is taken for granted. Just like when designing questionnaires, making the assumption that particular information is somehow 'shared' by those outside of a research team can often lead to research questions that fail to specify important aspects of a study.

There are certain aspects of empirical research that are common to nearly all research designs in social scientific investigations. These should always be considered when formulating research questions and information relating to these aspects of a study should always be made explicit within the questions, unless this information is redundant. The remainder of this section addresses these very aspects. The discussion is divided between the population of interest; the geographical location or coverage; the historical context; and the units of analysis and comparisons.

Population of interest

Specifying the population of interest answers the 'who' question posed by the commentators mentioned above. You should always remember, however, that a population of interest is not always composed of individual people. A population can be made up of groups, such as families, or institutions, such as schools or prisons. It can even be made up of events. The population of interest is important because it specifies the *coverage* of a study and contributes to an understanding of its scope.

It is important not to confuse the population of interest with the study sample. For reasons of time and cost most, but not all, empirical research collects data from a sample rather than from every relevant case. This *always* represents a compromise, however, and sampling should only be undertaken when the researcher is sure that population data is not available or could not realistically be collected with the resources available (Gorard 2003a).

In the example used above the population of interest is second-year medical students at Glasgow University. This population is relatively precisely defined and includes information about the type of individual the researchers are interested in ('medical students') and also the institution in which they are based ('Glasgow University'). It also limits the inquiry to students at a particular stage in their educational careers ('second year'). As it stands, however, this question does not differentiate between types of student, so the reader must assume that the population includes *all* medical students in their second year of studies at Glasgow University. This may include full-time and part-time students, 'standard-age' entrants and mature learners, and perhaps students enrolled on different courses aiming for a variety of qualifications in medicine.

As can be seen in the above example, being sufficiently specific about the population of interest is not straightforward. If the aims of a study really did require all second year students to be included in the research then the original formulation of the question would have adequately specified the population of interest. However, if this was not the case, additional information would need to be included.

Key Points

- Always make sure that your research questions contain information about your population of interest
- Populations are often made up of individual people but this is not always the case in social science research
- Remember not to confuse your population of interest with the sample from which you actually collect your data

---

Geographical location or coverage

In addition to specifying the population of interest precisely, it is also important to be explicit about the geographical coverage of the study. Even large-scale international studies are restricted in their scope and need to specify what regions *are*, and by implication *are not*, included in their research. It is sometimes the case that much of this information is contained in the specification of the population of interest, as in the above example. Because the population is restricted to students at the University of Glasgow we know that only students enrolled at this institution will participate in the research. However, this does not provide sufficient information about where these students reside. Some will undoubtedly live in Glasgow but others may commute from outside of the city and others may even be studying via distance learning.

The importance of this information will depend upon the aims of your study and the exact nature of each research question. As the study in the example relates to students' preferred learning environments, the institution in which they study is likely to be more relevant than their place of residence. A great deal of social research takes place within institutional settings such as schools, hospitals, prisons, workplaces, and so on, and such institutions often make up the 'cases' that are the focus of case-study research. It is not always the case, however, that the geographical boundaries of the research are set by the places where the data are collected. Sometimes these sites are chosen in order to conveniently access large numbers of relevant individuals or other cases, rather than because the researchers are interested in the sites themselves. Fieldwork often takes place in schools, for example, simply because it allows easy access to the majority of young people. However, not all of this research will relate directly, or even indirectly, to schools or even education.

Key Points

- Remember to include information in your research questions about the geographical coverage of your study
- This information might be obvious from your population of interest but this is not always the case

---

Historical context

Knowledge about the time period covered by a study is crucial for the interpretation of any research findings that are generated. Studies should ideally be located within a particular historical period in order for the findings to be appropriately contextualized. This 'when' is slightly different to the one used in the above example, which relates to biographical rather than historical time (Gorard & Rees 1999). The researchers are primarily concerned with the point at which students have reached during their academic career (i.e. 'second years') rather than the historical period in which the research took place. This focus of concern is not necessarily any less important, but relates more closely to the characteristics of the *population* of interest than to the historical context of a study.

It is important, however, not to confuse the historical period covered by a study with the period during which the fieldwork was conducted or data were collected. These may coincide but, depending on the topic under investigation, are often different. The *British Social Attitudes Survey*, for example, collects data on the current attitudes of participants to various aspects of social life and these data, by their very nature, correspond exactly with the time at which they were collected. In contrast, the life-history data collected as part of one of the research projects conducted as part of the *ESRC*'s 'Learning Society' programme was collected between 1996 and 1999 but covered events that occurred over 60 years previously (see Gorard & Rees 2002).

Although it is not always necessary or appropriate to include information about the time period covered by a study, you should consider the importance of this information when formulating your research questions. This may be of particular importance if the data cover a period before or after a major change in policy, or if they span a particular period of social change. The importance of the historical context of a study may not become apparent until after the research is completed, however, and therefore cannot be anticipated in all research questions. Nevertheless, considering this matter early on should ensure that any information about the historical coverage of a study is included in your research questions, where appropriate.

Key Points

- Include information about the time period covered by your study in your research questions if this is relevant.
- Don't confuse the time your data relate to with the time at which they were *collected*.

Comparisons

Most social research, by its very nature, involves comparisons (Bechhofer & Patterson 2000). These comparisons may be between individuals, social groups institutions or other units. They may be made over time or geographical area. When you are presented with data about a particular individual or group, you should always ask the question, 'Compared to what?'. This is particularly important given that a great deal of social research is concerned with measuring inequality, difference or change – concepts which, by definition, require comparisons to be made.

Deciding what comparisons should be made, however, is not always a straightforward matter (see Huff 1954, Paulos 2001, 1996, Brignell 2000, Best 2001, 2003, Gorard 2003a for detailed discussions and examples). Because of this, many data are presented without the appropriate comparative information, leading to both misinterpretations and erroneous claims. More often than not, this problem is caused by a failure on the part of the researchers to collect the relevant comparative data because they have not even realized that this was necessary.

Making comparisons explicit in research questions is a good way of ensuring that the appropriate comparators are included in a study, as they will be clear in the mind of the researcher from early on (Pole & Lampard 2002). This information is also useful to those reading research outputs and can aid the interpretation of the research findings and the evaluation of any conclusions drawn. The public often misinterpret media reports simply because journalists have failed to include the necessary comparative data (see Huff 1973, Brignell 2000, Best 2001, Gigerenzer 2003, Blastand & Dilnot 2007) and researchers need to ensure that they not only collect the appropriate data but also that they present it comprehensively, in a way that makes any comparisons made clear and explicit.

Key Points

- Think carefully about comparisons you will need to make in order to answer your research questions
- Always ask yourself, 'Compared to what?'
- Make sure that any comparisons you need to make are made explicit in your research questions

---

Your research questions should always contain sufficient information to convey precisely what your study intends to achieve and, as importantly, what it *does not*. Thinking about the issues discussed above will help clarify the nature and boundaries of your investigation and lay the groundwork for constructing a suitable research design. The inclusion of particular areas of information will depend, ultimately, on the nature of your particular research project and a degree of judgement is required in all such decisions.

Summary

This section has highlighted the importance of formulating research questions that are clear, concise and precise. While clarity and brevity are, to a certain extent, aspects of style, questions that are expressed clearly and in as few words as possible will communicate the purpose of the research much more clearly to readers. Additionally, the process of reformulating research questions helps the researcher to differentiate between the essential elements of an inquiry and those that are superfluous.

Deciding on the amount of information that needs to be included in a research question is a delicate balancing act, and the line between precision and redundancy is a fine one. The preceding discussion alerted readers to the kind of information that should be considered for inclusion in questions but exactly how much of this information is required will vary between research projects and will require researchers to exercise a degree of judgement.

Decisions relating to the scope of a research project cannot be made in a vacuum and you should always take into consideration the resources available for your study. The time and money you have at your disposal will have fundamental implications for the kind of research questions that you can realistically address. The next section examines the ways in which available resources can impact on research questions and draws attention to the various factors that must be considered when such questions are formulated.

A QUESTION OF RESOURCES

As has already been noted, when formulating your research questions it is important that you consider the resources available to you. You have to be realistic about what you can achieve given your personal circumstances and avoid the temptation to be over-ambitious. Ending up with a set of well-structured, well-written questions is pointless if you do not have the resources to conduct the research.

Resources relevant to the research process can be usefully divided into three types: funding, time and human resources. Although these resources are interrelated, for purposes of clarity they will be discussed separately. However, potential over-laps or trade-offs between resource types will be noted where relevant.

Funding and financial considerations

Most of the empirical research conducted by social scientists is funded by one of a large number of organizations in both the public and private sectors. In the United Kingdom, for example, the *Economic and Social Research Council* had a budget of £181 million to spend on social research in the academic year 2007/08, and funded projects conducted by over 2,500 professional researchers and more than 2,000 postgraduate students (ESRC 2007). In the United States, in 2005, the *National Science Foundation* dedicated a research budget of nearly $225 million to the social and behavioural sciences (Smith & Mathae 2004).

Professional researchers who apply to research councils for funding are usually required to prepare detailed costings and timetables in order to convince potential sponsors that the research is properly planned and can be realistically completed within budget. By the time they begin their research they will have already had to think about the scale of their project and the resources needed to address their research questions. They will have considered the financial costs of all aspects of their study in detail before applying for an appropriate level of funding.

In contrast, students conducting research projects will have little or no funding available to them to help with their research. While those studying for a PhD may have small allowances from their sponsors, self-funded doctoral students, masters students and undergraduates do not usually have any financial resources at their disposal. This can severely limit the kind of research that can be carried out and restrict the scope of a study.

As the sizeable research budgets of funding councils suggests, research can be an expensive business. It is common for research projects conducted by professional research teams to cost hundreds of thousands, if not millions, of pounds or dollars. If you are a student researcher with little in the way of financial resources, you will need to think through the potential cost of a study at the very beginning of the research process. This is because the nature of the research questions you formulate will have implications for the costs involved in conducting the research. If your research questions cannot be answered with the financial resources available to you, they will either need to be reformulated or abandoned altogether.

It can be difficult to anticipate exactly what costs are involved in any particular study. An accurate assessment of the potential costs of a research project cannot be made until issues of data collection and analysis have been fully thought through and a research design has been finalized. It is possible to anticipate some of the main areas where costs tend to be incurred during a research project, however, and these are outlined below. Their importance and relevance to a particular study will vary from case to case, depending on the research questions posed and the research design employed. Because of this, the following discussion cannot be comprehensive, but aims to highlight some of the potential costs of research rather than providing a definite checklist.

Travel and subsistence

Apart from human resources, which are discussed separately, travel and subsistence tend to be the most expensive outgoings for many research projects, particularly those involving a substantial amount of fieldwork. Researchers may need to travel to and from research sites many times, and these sites may be widely dispersed and/or situated a long way from the researcher's base. If extended periods in the field are required, 'subsistence' costs may also be accrued because of the need to purchase accommodation and meals.

Some research designs will clearly be more expensive than others with respect to travel and subsistence costs. Ethnographies can be expensive because of the sheer amount of time spent in the field, for example. Unless the research site is very local to the researcher, they may have to 'commute' on a daily basis for an extended period of time or even stay in accommodation local to the site of the fieldwork. Large-scale surveys can also be expensive if a wide geographical area must be covered and face-to-face administration of questionnaires or interviews is required.

There are ways in which some of these costs can be minimized, however, without unduly compromising the research design. Researchers conducting an ethnography can endeavour to find a suitable research site in their local area or, if this is not possible, as close as possible to where they are based. Conducting interviews or administering questionnaires using technologies such as telephones, email or the internet can also cut costs dramatically in survey research (but see Selwyn & Robson (1998) and Yun & Trumbo (2000) for the limitations of electronically administered surveys). A thorough and systematic search for existing secondary data can even remove the need to conduct a survey in the first place (Gorard 2003a, Smith 2008). Indeed, there are many ways in which the financially 'hard-pressed' researcher can cut travel and subsistence costs. As discussed below, however, the implications of any changes on the quality of the research should always be at the front of your mind.

The potential costs of travel and subsistence should be considered when research questions are formulated. Thinking through the implications of research questions in terms of the research design and methods of data collection that will be required can enable researchers to estimate the kind of costs that may be incurred in this area. Limiting the scope of various aspects of an investigation may be able to reduce such costs (see earlier discussion). However, if a particular research design is required to satisfactorily address the research questions that have been posed, it will not be possible to eliminate costs in this area completely without making fundamental changes to those questions.

Equipment

It is reasonably common for researchers to require at least some specialist equipment in order to conduct their research. This can range from relatively cheap items such as Dictaphones, used for recording interviews and focus groups, to very expensive pieces of technology such as video recorders and laptop computers. Specialist computer software, such as *SPSS* or *QSR NVivo*, is also often used to aid the process of data analysis. Sometimes optical equipment is used to read off data from fixed choice items on questionnaires.

As is the case with travel and subsistence costs, it is important to think carefully about any equipment that is required in order to conduct research. It is important to distinguish between equipment that is *essential* to the research design and that which is merely *desirable*. A cheap Dictaphone, for example, can be used instead of more expensive audio equipment, and many common statistical operations can be performed in *Microsoft Excel* if specialized statistical software is not available. While packages such as *QSR NVivo* can help with the analysis of textual or visual data, it is important to remember that it is the researcher – not the software – that conducts the analysis. Such analyses can be conducted perfectly adequately without using a computer and, moreover, there is by no means a consensus about the benefits of using this type of software (Bryman 2004).

Students and researchers based in university departments can often borrow equipment from their host institutions and often have access to specialist software when using campus-based computers. Other economical options include hiring essential equipment for the duration of the research. Thinking creatively about how research can be conducted, however, can often remove the need for expensive items, meaning the same results can be achieved for considerably less expense. Few research methods have been developed that are completely dependent on the use of high technology, so it is unlikely that your research plans will be thwarted completely.

Hidden costs

There are some costs that may not be immediately obvious to researchers beginning their first research project. Such costs can range from transcription costs for recorded interviews, through incentives for participants, to the costs of disseminating research findings. Because of the unpredictability of some of these costs, they cannot always be accurately assessed at the start of a project. It is important, however, that researchers anticipate the possibility of some of these hidden costs arising during the course of the research.

The transcription of interviews, from audio recordings to textual documents, is a time-consuming exercise. Because a single hour of audio tape can take more than eight hours to transcribe, and hundreds of hours of audio recordings can be produced over the course of a research project, this task is often contracted out to professional audio typists. While this saves the researcher a great deal of time, which can then be dedicated to other activities, it can also be very expensive. Student researchers can eliminate this expense simply by transcribing audio recordings themselves, although this can be a very time-consuming and tedious process.

Another cost that cannot always be foreseen is the need to offer participants financial incentives in order to secure their full cooperation. Evidence suggests that even small incentives can help minimize initial levels of non-response and drop-out during the course of the study (Bryman 2004) but even with small-scale studies the cumulative cost can be considerable. Alternative strategies, such as offering to provide respondents with research reports, can be more economical ways of increasing response rates, particularly when dealing with institutions.

Applications for research grants usually ask researchers to cost for 'consumables' when making a bid for funding. Office supplies and stationary are usually included under this heading, and in a small project are unlikely to cost a great deal. However, researchers planning to conduct a survey using postal questionnaires may find that the combined costs of stationary, photocopying and postage can be substantial. Expenditure in this area will vary from one research design to another but it is important that any costs are considered before the research progresses too far. Running out of postage when only half the questionnaires have been sent out will have serious consequences for a survey!

Dissemination

When planning a research project, it is easy to focus on conducting the actual research and neglect the crucial next stage of disseminating the findings. Students studying for undergraduate degrees are not usually required to present their work beyond their lecturers and fellow students, but postgraduate students should attempt to disseminate their research outputs as widely as possible. Organizations such as the *British Sociological Association, American Sociological Association* and *British Educational Research Association* organize special conferences where students can present their research to their peers. Such events can provide an opportunity to present a paper in a setting that is less intimidating than regular conferences, with the added advantage of disseminating your work to a wider audience. However, there is usually a charge for attending these conferences, and also the added cost of transport and accommodation to consider.

Researchers planning to apply for funding from research councils are advised to consider the many ways in which their findings can be disseminated, and to budget for these. Newsletters, working papers, websites and dedicated conferences can all be used to disseminate research findings but the nature of the research questions will dictate the audience(s) for whom the research will be relevant. Those planning research that will be relevant to policy-makers and practitioners may want to consider setting up proprietary dissemination strategies for each different audience.

Training

It is sometimes necessary to undertake additional training in order to use a particular method of data collection or analysis, or use a specific computer software package. As has already been discussed, research questions should initially be formulated without being restricted by a researcher's existing skills or preferences (Mason 1996, Denscombe 2003) and researchers should be open to the possibility of using new and unfamiliar techniques. Many aspects of research methods can be learned on short training courses with minimum disruption to the progress of a study, and training budgets are often included in doctoral scholarships or small research grants. A question should not be deemed 'unresearchable' if the only barrier is a lack of skills in a particular area and it is possible for the researcher, or a member of the research team, to develop the skills that are required.

Key Points

- Remember that research is expensive and that you have limited resources
- Don't be too ambitious in terms of either the scope or scale of your project
- Think about the costs of travel, equipment, consumables and training
- Revise your research questions if your study is likely to be beyond your means

---

There is no simple equation that means more money leads to better research (Denscombe 2002). Important research can be conducted on a shoe-string and multi-million pound projects do not necessarily produce useful findings. It is vital, however, that the research questions you pose can be addressed given the resources at your disposal.

Ensuring that the research questions are 'researchable' in terms of the financial resources available may just be a matter of reducing the scale of a project in terms of the population of interest or geographical or historical coverage. In some cases, the scope and direction of an investigation may need to be changed. However, there is always the possibility that an entire project may have to be abandoned, or at least temporarily shelved, simply because it is too costly.

The resources available to researchers should not only be viewed in financial terms, however. The time available to conduct a study can also limit the kinds of questions that are asked, or at least the form they finally take. The size of a research team, or the number of people willing to help the researcher, should also be considered.

Time and human resources

The time available to conduct the research is one of the most important considerations when formulating research questions and designing a research strategy. As frequently noted in this book, there is a tendency for inexperienced researchers to be over-ambitious in their estimations of what questions can be addressed given the constraints they face.

Different research methods can be time consuming in different, and sometimes unexpected ways. For example, while interviews can sometimes be conducted with relatively little preparation they are very time consuming to transcribe and analyse. Questionnaires, on the other hand, are often quick and simple to analyse but require multiple drafts, and can take considerable time to pre-pilot and then pilot. The results of randomized controlled trials (RCTs) can also be relatively simple to analyse but require a great deal of preparation and often require data collection to continue over a lengthy period of time. Given the widespread practice of archiving data electronically, existing secondary data sets can be obtained very quickly and easily, and often downloaded direct to the researcher's personal computer. However, a considerable amount of 'data husbandry' is often required before this information can be analysed (Smith 2008).

The choice of research design also has implications for the time needed to complete a project. Longitudinal studies, by their very nature, require time to pass between periods of data collection (although the amount of time required will vary according to the objectives of a study). Research relying on cross-sectional data will usually be less time-consuming but the time needed will, again, depend on exactly what questions are being addressed.

It is important to draw up a timetable when planning your research and less experienced researchers should seek the advice of more experienced colleagues in order to assess whether this timetable is realistic. If this is judged not to be the case, modifications need to be made either to the research design, the research questions, or both. This timetable should cover all stages of the research process, from planning, through data collection and analysis, to dissemination. It is important to consider the amount of time that can actually be dedicated to a study and not to ignore other study or work commitments.

Research questions and resources

An idea that is returned to repeatedly in this book is that developing research questions is an iterative process. Research questions tend to be formulated and developed before being reformulated in response to a number of considerations. One such consideration should be the resources available for the research. After initially generating a set of research questions and modifying them until they are coherent and well focused (see above), the next stage of the research process is to design a research strategy. As is discussed in Chapter 4, thinking about the kind of data that are required to answer the research questions satisfactorily is often the best place to start this process. This naturally leads to a consideration of the methods of data collection that are best suited to generating these data, and types of analysis that will be required to make sense of the data. By this point, and without having to outline the research design in great detail, some indication of the resource implications of the research questions will emerge. The extent to which these questions are 'researchable' given the constraints on resources can then be assessed.

If there is a mismatch between the available resources and the resources needed to address the research questions, the researcher must choose between one of two courses of action. They can either seek additional resources, perhaps by applying for a research grant, or can reframe 'the question so that it can be satisfactorily answered within the existing constraints' (Stone 2002, p. 267). The latter course of action is much more common and will usually be the only realistic option for student researchers.

SUMMARY

As was discussed in Chapter 1, it is important to be able to distinguish between questions that can be addressed by empirical research and those that cannot. Before proceeding any further, the researcher needs to establish that the research questions they have initially generated are researchable 'in principle'. If this is not the case, they should either be modified appropriately or, if this is not possible, discarded. When a set of research questions have been formulated that clearly and unambiguously meet this requirement, it is then necessary to develop and refine them further to ensure they are researchable 'in practice'.

Research questions play a vital role in directing and focusing the research. Questions should clearly indicate what the research aims to achieve and what it does not. It is important that questions are formulated in a way that effectively 'bounds' the study, thus providing readers, and reminding researchers, exactly what topics the research intends to address. It is important to limit the scope of *any* research project, both to ensure it can be carried out given the resources available, and to provide sufficient direction to construct an appropriate research design.

Placing research questions in order of priority and organizing them into hierarchies of main and subsidiary questions can be a useful way of both reducing the number of questions and tightening the focus of a study. Taking care of the way questions are worded can also help set the parameters of the research and prepare the ground for constructing a research design. As a general rule, questions should be stated as briefly as possible and should be free from all unnecessary jargon. They should communicate the research objectives precisely and explicitly and include all necessary information relating to the population of interest, geographical and temporal coverage, units of analysis and comparators.

It will always be necessary to strike a balance between the scope of a study and the resources available to the researcher. Funding, time and human resources must be considered at all times but the study should not be restricted by existing preferences and skills in data collection and analysis. Researchers should always be looking to develop their skills and expertise and, where possible, research projects should be used as opportunities to engage in professional development.

Research questions can be altered in quite subtle ways if it becomes apparent, on close inspection, that they cannot be adequately addressed with the resources at your disposal. The scope of a research project can be narrowed simply by reducing the number of questions being addressed or by modifying or removing key terms in particular questions. It is important not to be over-ambitious about the kind of questions that can be addressed in a single study; it is far better to thoroughly and comprehensively answer a few well-defined questions than to provide inadequate answers to a wide range of very broad questions.

The importance of the links between research questions and research design have been mentioned frequently over the course of this chapter and, indeed, throughout the chapters that preceded it. The following chapter addresses this matter in greater depth before the issue of answering questions is taken up, in Chapter 5.

FURTHER READING

Kane provides a useful and well-illustrated discussion of the importance of defining key terms in your research questions:

Kane, E. (1984) *Doing Your Own Research: Basic Descriptive Research in the Social Sciences and Humanities*. London: Marion Boyars.

Bechhofer and Patterson outline in detail the importance of comparison (and control) in the research process:

Bechhofer, F. & Patterson, L. (2000) *Principles of Research Design in the Social Sciences*. London: Routledge. ch. 1.

4 Questions, methods and indicators

In the first three chapters, I have repeatedly tried to stress the importance of the connection between research questions and research design, and have argued that the design and methods you use should follow logically from the questions you are attempting to answer. The first part of this chapter examines this issue in some detail, and explores some of the dangers of method-led, rather than question-led, research. The differences between research design and methods of data collection and analysis are discussed briefly, and the need for researchers to think carefully about the *design* of their study, regardless of the questions being addressed, is reiterated.

The remainder of the chapter addresses one of the most important stages of development when moving from thinking about research questions to considering issues of data collection. Having defined important concepts in your research (see Chapter 2) it is necessary to operationalize these concepts via the use of particular indicators. This vital part of the research process is explored in detail through the use of worked examples.

QUESTIONS AS THE STARTING POINT OF RESEARCH

In addition to being clear about exactly what your research aims to accomplish, having precise and well-written research questions helps the researcher plan a coherent research design. Well-formulated research questions promote clarity of thought, thereby informing the choice of research design (Stone 2002) and being clear about the purpose of the research 'streamlines' the production of a suitable research design (Denscombe 2002). Once an appropriate research design has been constructed, the researcher can then decide upon suitable methods of data collection and analysis.

Spending time developing and refining research questions pays dividends later in the research process, when making decisions about research design, and data collection and analysis, as such decisions will be helped greatly by a coherent set of well-formulated questions. This is because a clearly formulated research question will indicate exactly what data will be necessary to answer it (Punch 1998). Indeed, thinking about what data is required to address a question should be the first step in moving from research question to research design (de Vaus 2001).

Research questions should focus the research 'both in terms of its substantive content and the data-collection methods which are likely to prove most successful in seeking answers to them' (Pole & Lampard 2002, p. 13). Research questions that do not suggest exactly what data are required to answer them need to be re-written until this 'empirical criterion' is met (Punch 1998). If you do not know exactly what kind of evidence is required to answer your research questions, you will be unable to choose the most appropriate research design and methods of data collection and analysis. As is discussed in the following section, questions about methods must necessarily *follow* questions about data, which in turn follow from the research questions themselves.

Questions first, methods later

At the beginning of your study, thinking about research questions should always take priority over thinking about research methods (Lundstedt 1968). As Punch (1998, p. 21) notes 'we first need to establish what we are trying to find out, and then consider how we are going to do it'. The researcher's first priority should always be 'carefully thinking through what he or she wants to learn', as studies with poorly thought out questions are at least as common as those with sound questions but inappropriate research designs (Locke et al. 2004, p. 130).

As was discussed in Chapter 1, you should always start with questions and, at least at the outset, not constrain your thinking about *what* you want to find out by thinking too much about *how* this will be achieved. You can initially proceed with the assumption that there will be methods suitable for whatever questions they end up with (Punch 1998). You should certainly not give in to the temptation to choose your research questions to fit with the methods of data collection and analysis that you are most comfortable using (Mason 1996).

The issue of linking research questions to data collection and analysis is returned to later in this chapter, where it is explored in greater detail. Before this, however, a number of issues relating to the choice of methods and research design are discussed, in order to dispel some of the most common misconceptions in this area. The inter-related topics of research 'traditions', methods-led research and the role of research design in 'qualitative' research are addressed directly below.

Key Points

- Thinking about research questions should always come before thinking about research methods
- Don't become too preoccupied with methods in the very early stages of your study – concentrate on getting your questions right first

---

Research 'traditions'

In the current and recent methods literature, a great deal of attention has been devoted to the discussion of 'traditions' in data collection and analysis. These discussions often unhelpfully polarize caricatured versions of 'interpretivism' and 'positivism' (see Halfpenny (1982) for a discussion of the problems with defining the latter) and frequently suggest that novice researchers identify with one side or another. Debates about the relative merits of supposedly alternative approaches have often been couched as 'epistemological' in nature but the differences are more accurately characterized as technical rather than philosophical (Bryman 1988, Robson 1993). Stone (2002, p. 256) supports the view that the focus of these debates is misplaced, arguing that 'the question being asked determines the appropriate research architecture, strategy and tactics to be used – not tradition, authority, experts, paradigms or schools of thought'.

According to Denscombe (2002), however, there has been a move away from dogmatic attachment to these 'traditions' towards a pragmatic approach to social research, evident in the growing tendency to combine research methods and for researchers to become eclectic in their choice of methods (see also Tashakkori & Teddlie 1998). The guiding principle for much contemporary research, he argues, 'is not how well it sticks to its "positivist" or "interpretivist" epistemology, but how well it addresses the topic it is investigating' (Denscombe 2003, p. 23). Whether research has ever been judged according to these criteria is debatable. What is clear however, is that a great deal of research continues to be led by methods rather than by questions, a phenomenon that has caused considerable concern in some quarters.

Students and new researchers should be wary of immediately identifying themselves with particular research traditions, however tempting a certain approach might appear. Forming an identity shaped by a predilection for particular research methods or research designs will tend to limit the kind of questions that a researcher is prepared, or able, to address. Such identities tend to persist for the remainder of a researcher's career and are central to the production and maintenance of 'mono-methods' research (Gorard 2002a). As is discussed in the next section, this is not conducive to a healthy and vibrant research community (Campbell et al. 1982, Dillon 1984).

Preoccupation with debates surrounding these traditions can also lead to unnecessary concern with philosophical debates about ontology and epistemology (what it is possible to know about the world and this knowledge can be obtained). As noted above, these debates are often less relevant than some commentators suggest, and can distract attention from more important issues. Although some authors (e.g. Mason 1996) believe students should *start* by figuring out their ontological and epistemological positions, this is likely to confuse and distract inexperienced researchers and is certainly not something I would recommend. Indeed, some very successful researchers believe that such debates can be ignored completely, with no negative consequences for the quality of research output. As a general rule, students and new researchers need not concern themselves too much with such debates, as their connections with the actual conduct of research is frequently exaggerated (Bryman 1988).

Key Points

- The philosophical links made between research 'traditions' and the use of particular research methods are often exaggerated
- Do not feel that you have to identify yourself with a particular 'tradition' before you start any research – it will not necessarily make you a better researcher
- Don't worry if you don't understand some of the epistemological debates presented in some texts. It is possible to conduct high-quality research without understanding these philosophical issues

---

Methods-led research and 'methodolatry'

Many experienced researchers and stakeholders in both Campbell et al.'s (1982) and Taylor (2002) surveys expressed the concern that far too much research is led by preferences for certain methods or techniques rather than the desire to answer a particular question. According to many of the successful and highly regarded researchers in Campbell et al.'s (1982) study, the driving force behind most significant 'research milestones' tended to be specific problems to be addressed rather than the use of particular methods. However, a survey of the educational research literature, published only two years later, suggested that the reality was far removed from what was viewed as best practice. The author concluded that, at least in one major field of social scientific research, 'inquiries appear *not* to be characterized by the formulation of questions for study' (Dillon 1984, p. 24). Both authors view this situation as problematic, with Dillon (1984, p. 335) warning that 'the identification of questions according to research method may yield a restricted range of questions for study', and Campbell et al. (1982) expressing concern that the repeated use of the same methods led to the creation of 'research ruts'.

Two decades after Campbell et al.'s (1982) and Dillon's (1984) studies, the stakeholders in Taylor's (2002) survey expressed similar anxieties, with particular concern being focused on 'mono-method' researchers, who repeatedly use a single or narrow range of research methods and/or research designs. The director of a large grant awarding body supported the view that research should start with questions, stating: 'I think on balance it's a good thing to be problem driven. What did they say about single methodology people – give a child a hammer and everything becomes a nail' (Taylor 2002, p. 58).

Janesik (2000, p. 390) uses the term 'methodolatry' to describe the 'slavish attachment and devotion to method' that can lead to methods coming before questions in social research. Attachment to, or preference for, particular methods of data collection or analysis restricts the scope of inquiry because it allows 'a pre-decision on method or technique to decide the question to be asked' (Robson 1993, p. 28). Indeed, the tendency to use the same research methods or research designs throughout their careers is not restricted to any particular research 'tradition'. It is common for researchers to define themselves in terms of their preferred methods of data collection or analysis, regardless of their particular area of expertise. While some researchers define themselves as 'ethnographers', 'case-study researchers' or 'conversational analysts', others happily describe themselves as 'ANOVA researchers' (Miles & Shevlin 2001) or 'multi-level modellers'. This leads to the construction and maintenance of 'mono-methods' identities which, as well as limiting professional development and hindering the production of 'compleat' researchers, work against question-led or problem-focused research (Gorard 2002a).

Another problem symptomatic of the tendency to place methods before questions is the infatuation with fashionable 'technical gimmicks' (Medawar 1979, p. 15). An example of this is the widespread use of multi-level statistical modelling (also referred to as 'hierarchical linear modelling', see Goldstein (2003)), a complex technique that has yet to be proven to be superior to more simple and readily understandable methods of analysis (Coe &

Fitz-Gibbon 1998, Fitz-Gibbon 2000, 2001, Mitchell 2001, Gorard 2003b, 2007). This technique has often been used instead of more simple, and more widely understood, analytic techniques, sometimes to the detriment of the quality of the research (see Gorard 2003c).

Robson (1993, p. 28) notes an interesting variant of this phenomenon, whereby research questions are developed simply because they allow the research to use a particular computer software package for statistical analysis. He views this as 'almost a big a research sin as designing and carrying out a study that you don't know how to analyse'. Indeed, it is important for researchers not to fetishize computer software and over-estimate its contribution to the process of data analysis. Packages such as *SPSS* have undoubtedly made statistical analyses easier and quicker to conduct, and enabled complex analyses to be conducted by a wider range of researchers. It is still necessary, however, for those using such software to have a solid conceptual understanding of the procedures they are carrying out, to be clear about the rationale for any analytic decisions they make, and to be confident in their ability to interpret the output of the analyses they conduct.

There are also important issues relating to the use of the more recently developed software intended to assist with the analysis of textual and visual data. Packages such as *NUD*IST, NVivo* or *Atlas.ti* are often employed by researchers when analysing large bodies of interview data, for example. They are primarily organizational tools but it is common for research reports to suggest that the data were somehow analysed by the software *itself*. It is by no means necessary to use computer software to analyse textual or visual data, however, and these packages only replicate processes that can be conducted manually, with pen and paper (and even glue and scissors). They do not, and cannot, replace any of the intellectual activity involved in conducting analysis. Just like statistical packages, they do not take the place of the researcher's judgement.

Many commentators seem to agree that methods-led research is a less than ideal approach to social research, yet the available empirical evidence cited above suggests that this practice is widespread. Indeed, evidence of the repeated use of a very narrow range of methods of data collection and analysis can easily be found in the past publications of many well-known and highly regarded researchers. While this is not strictly evidence of methods-led research *per se*, it does raise questions about *why*, if this is not the case, researchers spend entire careers investigating only a narrow range of question types.

It is easy to see the attraction of the 'mono-method' approach, as it provides the researcher with the security of relying on existing skills they are already comfortable using. However, it is ultimately very restrictive in terms of the types of questions that can be addressed, at least by a single researcher, and is therefore incompatible with a genuinely curiosity-led approach to research. Restricting your knowledge to a narrow range of research designs, methods and analytic techniques also has implications for scholarship, particularly in relation to the ability to critically engage with their colleagues' work (Gorard 2003a).

New researchers are advised to be open-minded and adventurous in relation to the methods of data collection and analysis that they are prepared to use. There is no reason why any research design, method of data collection or analytic technique should be ruled out unless it is unsuitable for the task at hand. Inexperienced researchers will necessarily have to learn new skills in order to conduct research but the truly curious researcher should be willing to learn *any* new research design, or method of data collection or analysis, in order to answer the question that drives their research. Neither should the acquisition of new research skills be restricted to those at the beginning of their research skills. There is no reason why researchers should not continue to expand their repertoire of methods over the course of their careers, even if this is not currently the norm.

While methods-led, or at least methods-restricted, research is commonplace in social science, this is far from a desirable situation. The increased use of large research teams ameliorates the problems caused by such approaches, but the individual researcher, working alone, has none of the benefits that working in a team can offer. Individuals who consciously restrict the types of methods and designs they will use inevitably limit the types of research questions they can address. And even those working with a team would benefit from wider understanding of different approaches, as this would enable them to contribute to a wider range of discussions and reduce the degree to which they abdicate decision-making to others or accept particular views 'on trust'.

In either case, research is a much more useful and meaningful activity if it is led by questions or problems, rather than research-ers' preferences for particular methods, designs or techniques. It should be recognized that the present situation exists as a research culture, rather than being based on reasoned argument or evidence to suggest its efficacy. New researchers should not be intimidated by the existing *status quo* and are advised to take a question-led approach, safe in the knowledge that this position is more easily defensible than the practise of some of their more experienced colleagues.

Key Points

- Your research should be driven by the desire to answer particular research questions, not by preferences for particular methods of data collection and analysis.
- Don't restrict the focus of your research by only using research methods you have previously employed. Be open-minded about learning new skills.
- Using very complex analytical techniques or state-of-the-art soft-ware packages will not necessarily improve your analysis.

THE IMPORTANCE OF RESEARCH DESIGN

Formulating research questions and constructing a research design around them have sometimes been viewed as processes that are only necessary in certain types of research. Some of those working in the 'qualitative' research tradition have resisted the idea that all studies must begin with research questions and a corresponding research design, suggesting that this is only necessary in so-called 'quantitative' research (Mason 1996). However, these elements of the research process are central to *all* studies, regardless of the methods of data collection or analysis employed (Flick 1998,

Sarantakos 1998). Even in studies where questions are expected to develop over the course of the research, investigators should be clear about what they want to study (Jorgenson 1989). And Denscombe (2002, p. 112) reminds us that 'there are no good grounds for qualitative research to excuse itself from the criteria for good research that apply to other social science approaches'.

Although it would be unrealistic to aim to cover even a fraction of the issues necessary to acquaint the reader with the principles of research design, a central aim of this chapter is to make the important link between research questions and research design and to outline the essential process of operationalizing key concepts. Once you have reached this stage of an investigation, it will be necessary either to consult colleagues or teachers who are experienced in designing research projects or to refer to texts available in this area. I recommend de Vaus's (2001) excellent text, although Hakim's (2000) well-known text is also useful.

What is research design?

Research design is the point at which research questions are converted into research projects (Hakim 2000). It marks the stage in the research process when the researcher moves from thinking about asking questions to thinking in detail about how these questions might be answered. The essence of developing a research design is making decisions about the kinds of evidence required to address your research question (de Vaus 2001). It is not about *how* to conduct research – the research methods – but rather about the *logic* of inquiry; the links between questions, data and conclusions.

Although they are often confused, research designs and methods of data collection are separate issues (de Vaus 2001) and there are no necessary links between the two. As de Vaus (2001, p. 16) notes, 'any research design can, in principle, use any type of data collection and can use either qualitative or qualitative data'. He emphasizes the primacy of research design over research methods by arguing that 'in social research the issues of sampling, method of data collection (e.g. questionnaire, observation, document analysis) [and] design of questions are all subsidiary to the matter of "What evidence do I need to collect?"' (p. 9).

Both Hakim (2000) and de Vaus (2001) use the analogy of constructing a building to illustrate the difference between research design and methods of data collection. Constructing a research design is akin to the drawing up the blueprints for a building and the role of the researcher at this stage is thus similar to that of an architect. This role is distinct from that of actually constructing the building, a task that is undertaken by bricklayers, carpenters, electricians, and so on. In the analogy, the construction work is comparable to the collection of data by researchers working in the field.

Research design 'deals primarily with aims, uses, purposes, intentions and plans' (Hakim 2000, p. 1) but 'a research design is *not* just a work plan' (de Vaus 2001, p. 9). As Yin (1989, p. 29) argues, research design 'deals with a *logical* problem and not a *logistical* problem'. The logical problem is to work out what kind of data is needed to address the research questions most directly and provide an answer that can be defended by reference to the evidence collected.

De Vaus (2001) divides research designs into four categories: experimental designs, longitudinal designs, cross-sectional designs and case-study designs. Which design, or combination of designs, you use will depend on the nature of your research questions. For example, if you were concerned with describing how rates of criminal convictions have changed over time, you would need a cross-sectional design, as you would require data on crime rates at different points in history. Alternatively, if you wanted to ascertain the effectiveness of an initiative aimed at increasing rates of recycling, you would need an experimental design, because you would need to compare the changes in rates of recycling in areas that experienced the initiative with those in areas that did not. And if you are examining how people's learning habits change over their lifetime, you would need a longitudinal design. As these examples show, research design is less about how you will collect your data, and more about the type of data that needs to be collected in order to address your research questions.

OPERATIONALIZING CONCEPTS

Before you move on to constructing a research design, it is often necessary to define and operationalize some of the concepts in your research questions. The importance of clearly defining the key terms in your research question was discussed in Chapter 3. Once you have done this, you will then need to think about exactly what kind of data you will need to answer your questions. Before you can do this, however, you will need to 'operationalize' some of the key concepts and variables included in your research questions. Operationalization is the process of transforming a concept or variable from an abstract idea into something that can be researched. In short, it should provide 'clear and specific instructions on what and how to observe' (Kerlinger 1973, p. 32). If all the concepts and variables in your research questions are clearly defined and operationalized, it should be reasonably straightforward for you to work out what kind of data you need to collect in your study and then construct an appropriate research design.

In everyday life, we often take the links between concepts and the things they represent for granted because these concepts have already been operationalized for us. We can make measurements of the dimensions of an object, for example, without needing to think about the theoretical links between the concepts of height, length and width and the data we are collecting. The scales we use to make such measurements – whether imperial, metric or otherwise – are arbitrary social constructs developed for our convenience (Prandy 2002). Metres and centimetres have no independent existence but are merely tools we have created to help us in our daily lives. It is only because they are universally accepted and widely used that we tend not to question the links between these scales and the physical properties of the objects we are interested in measuring.

The concepts we are most interested in as social scientists tend to differ from the above example in two important respects. First, while there may be some agreement about the importance of many concepts (such as social class) there tends to be much less agreement on their definition and even greater disagreement about how they should be operationalized. Berg (2004) gives the examples of 'quality of life' and 'religiosity' as two concepts that might interest social scientists but which present difficulties when it comes to definition and operationalization. We may think we know what we mean when we say that someone is 'very religious' but it is difficult to come up with ways to differentiate between the religiosity of particular individuals or groups.

One of the ways in which social scientists attempt to operationalize the concepts they are interested in is through the use of 'indicators'. Because the kind of measures and scales we use to find out about the physical world simply do not exist for many of the social phenomena we wish to research, it is often necessary to collect information that is *related to* that phenomena. So while we could easily and accurately measure an individual's height, it is much more challenging to provide an assessment of their health. Data on their height could be collected using a number of instruments, such as a tape measure or a ruler, and could be communicated to others using either metric or imperial units of length. Unfortunately, no such scales or instruments can provide the same simple output relating to an individual's health. However, we could collect data relating to their biography and behaviour that can serve as 'indicators' of their current state of health. These might include number of days absent from work due to ill-health, visits to the doctor or hospital in the past year, episodes of major illness in the past five years, self-reports of subjective feelings of well-being, and so on. Based on the information provided by these indicators, we might then rank individuals or assign them to categories in order to differentiate between those who were in better or worse states of health.

This kind of approach is not without its problems, however. It is important to remember at all times that it is not actually the concept itself that is being measured but only behaviour or events that are approximately related to it. It is vital that you are clear what indicators are being used and, in the case of multiple indicators, how they are being combined to discriminate between individuals or groups.

As can be seen from the present discussion, moving from definitions to indicators can be a difficult and thought-provoking process. It is important to reiterate that thinking about how concepts are to be operationalized is necessary *whatever type of research is being conducted*. Researchers conducting 'qualitative' studies need to pay just as much attention to these issues as those intending to carry out quantitative analysis (Denscombe 2002). The key consideration is what counts as evidence for the existence of a particular phenomenon, not whether numeric values are to be assigned to cases for the purposes of analysis.

It is common for researchers to encounter problems when defining key concepts and attempting to identify or develop suitable indicators to use in their research. If these difficulties become insurmountable, however, it may be necessary to return to your research questions and reconsider the role of these concepts in your study. As discussed in Chapter 2, some phenomena cannot be studied meaningfully simply because it is impossible to collect relevant data. Alternatively, it might be the case that while relevant data could be collected in theory, the practical limitations of your circumstances prevent you from doing this.

Key Points

- It is important that you operationalize the key concepts and variables included in your research questions
- Some concepts will be more difficult to operationalize than other and some may be impossible to operationalize effectively
- The most important consideration is to be clear and transparent about the definitions and indicators you use

---

To illustrate the problems faced by researchers when attempting to operationalize concepts central to their research, the example of social class is discussed in detail below. This example was chosen both because of its common use and application in social scientific disciplines and because it illustrates many of the difficulties faced by researchers relating to operationalization and measurement.

An example of a social scientific concept: social class

Many studies, particularly those concerned with inequalities, aim to discover whether particular social phenomenon are related to social class. Along with gender, age, ethnicity and geographic location, social class is one of the most common contextual variables used in social research.

When social class is discussed in everyday life or in the media, it is often treated as if its meaning and measurement were straightforward and, at least for the purpose of most informal debates, assuming a shared meaning is relatively unproblematic. However, social scientists, and their audiences, need to be completely clear about how concepts such as 'social class' are both defined and operationalized. While this may sound relatively simple, the way in which this is achieved has been the subject of a great deal of dispute in the social science community for many years (see Crompton 1998). A researcher interested in social class faces a number of difficult decisions relating to how social class is defined, how class groups are differentiated, and what data are required in order to allocate individuals to different class categories.

Exactly what data need to be collected to establish a person's social class depends on how class is defined and subsequently operationalized. Data on an individual's occupational status are commonly used but other types of information, on income and education for example, are sometimes included, especially when multiple indicators are used. Sometimes data are collected at the family, rather than individual, level and young people under the age of 18 may be classified according to their parents' position.

Defining and operationalizing social class can be a very difficult exercise, and it is not surprising that some social scientists have devoted their entire careers to this project. Because of this, however, several class schema have been developed specifically to be used by the wider social science community. Crompton (1998) provides a useful comparison of some of the more commonly used schema, and her text serves as an ideal starting point for researchers new to the area. The more recently developed *National Statistics Socio-economic Classification*, designed to replace those previously used by the *Office for National Statistics*, has the advantage of comparability with government statistics and is also worth considering (see Rose & Pevalin 2003).

The easiest and safest option for inexperienced researchers is to use an existing schema. It is important that you state explicitly which schema you are using and follow the guidelines on its proper use. Unless you have considerable expertise, I would not recommend taking a piecemeal approach to the adoption of a particular schema or to attempt to 'tinker' with existing classifications.

Collecting the data necessary to ascertain an individual's social class can be very challenging in some studies. Researchers using existing secondary data sets are often frustrated by the lack of data relevant to this area (Smith 2008) and those working with young people frequently face difficulties obtaining data relating to the family backgrounds of research participants. You should carefully consider the likelihood of being able to obtain certain data *before* you have settled on a particular class schema, as the success of your study will depend on access to the relevant information. Other factors, such as comparability with other research in the field, might also be important. While relatively simple measures such as the *Registrar General's* classification have been criticized by some class analysts, they often require much less information than other, more theoretically developed classifications, and their widespread use gives them the advantage of comparability. It has also been noted that, in any case, the final classifications are not vastly different from those produced using many of the 'sociological' schema (Crompton 1998).

If it seems unlikely that sufficient data will be available to classify individuals according to social class, it may be necessary to use a different variable in your research questions. This will inevitably change the nature of your study but may represent a sensible compromise between the original aims and the available data. Broader measures such as 'status', for example, can be useful, if less precise, alternatives (Crompton 1998).

It is also necessary to consider matters relating to data analysis when choosing a suitable schema. For example, if your planned sample or population for a study is necessarily very small, you would be unwise to use a classification scheme that had a large minimum number of class categories, as the distribution of a small number of cases over a relatively large number of categories is likely to hinder any useful comparative analysis. In contrast, in large samples or populations with similar socio-economic backgrounds, it may be necessary to make quite subtle distinctions between class backgrounds, and thus a schema with a large number of finely differentiated categories may be required.

The eventual decision regarding the most appropriate schema should be the result of a process of considerable deliberation. The aims of the study should be considered alongside the kinds of data likely to be available and the analyses that are required. Taking time to proceed in this way will mean that you will have had to plan important aspects of both the process of data collection and subsequent analysis, reducing the risks of encountering problems later in the research. Each important concept and variable relating to the research questions should be treated in the same way.

This kind of attention to detail and forward planning is certainly not a universal aspect of many research projects. Many experienced researchers fail to think carefully about operationalizing the variables in their studies even when, as in the case of social class, an abundance of advice is available in the existing literature. For example, the interview schedule used in Ainley and Bailey's (1997, p. 132) study of students' experiences of further education included the following question:

> *Would you call yourself working class, middle class or any other class, or don't you think of yourself like that?*

While there was no explicit class analysis in the research report, neither was there an indication that this question was merely used to gather data on students' perceptions of their class background. It is used here as an example of a question that would be unsuitable for gathering data on class as it makes the mistake of confusing a research question with a data collection question (see Chapter 2). If a researcher is interested in a participant's social class, they should seek to collect the relevant background data required by the classification they are using; they should not ask the participant to classify themselves.

A different, but equally problematic, mistake is made by Ball et al. (2000), in their study of young people's post-16 transitions. While the authors make much of the 'classed' nature of choice in their conclusions, at no point do they discuss what they mean by 'class', or how it was operationalized and measured in their study (see White 2007). Because of this omission it is very difficult to assess whether their conclusions are justified and, if so, what the implications of their findings would be.

Like many social scientific concepts, social class can be difficult to define and operationalize. Many commonly used concepts in social science face similar problems, often because of a lack of agreement about their meaning. But while Jevons (1874, p. 77) warns that 'there must generally be an unlimited number of modes of classifying a group of objects' there are ways in which researchers can guard themselves against criticism for the way they have defined and operationalized a particular concept. Being explicit and transparent about the reasons for choosing a particular classification, and justifying this choice in terms of the aims of the research should always provide a robust defence against any attacks. And as with most aspects of research, supplying the readers and consumers of research with sufficient information to make their own judgements should be a priority at all stages of the research process.

Unoperational concepts

Some concepts, whilst initially appearing to be useful, are particularly difficult to operationalize in any meaningful way, and therefore are of limited use to social researchers. As was noted in Chapter 3, the more abstract a concept, the more challenging it will be to define and operationalize effectively. Researchers should think very carefully about any concepts they include in their research questions, however common they are in the wider literature.

Researching the incidence of respiratory illness among school children, for example, will be easier than attempting to assess their general health, because the first concept is more specific, easier to define, and therefore fairly straightforward in terms of operationlization via specific indicators. As was discussed earlier in this chapter, assessing the general 'health' of an individual would be much more challenging because of the breadth of coverage of this concept, the lack of consensus about how it should be defined, and problems with the use and combination of the large number of indicators that could be used. Similarly, and for the same reasons, it is much easier to measure educational test scores than it is to provide an overall assessment of 'intelligence' or even general educational aptitude.

The problem for social scientists is that we are sometimes very interested in finding out about the health of the nation or the educational abilities of our school children. When this is the case, we need to think carefully about how we operationalize these concepts and be transparent about the definitions and indicators we use. It is also important to be explicit about the limitations of any measures we develop or employ.

As discussed earlier, it is important to be clear about which concepts are essential elements of a research question and which ones are dispensable. It is relatively common for researchers to be seduced into including fashionable theoretical ideas in their research, either explicitly, in their research questions, or as *post factum* explanations of their findings. However tempting this may be, the implications for operationalization and measurement should always be thought through, especially if the intention is to provide a rigorous test of a particular theoretical construct. If such a test is not being carried out, the role of the particular theoretical construct in the research should be questioned (see Chapter 1).

Examples of commonly used, but problematic, theoretical constructs are discussed below, in order to illustrate how issues of definition and operationalization are often neglected by researchers working in a wide range of substantive areas. The particular examples have been chosen because they are used in a wide range of social science disciplines, and because of the frequency of their recent use. Many other examples could have been chosen, but those described below adequately illustrate the potential problems with these ideas.

The concept of economic capital has been used in economics for many years and is relatively easy to operationalize, as it is defined and measured in monetary terms. However, in the last quarter of the twentieth century the term 'capital' was borrowed from this original context and used a metaphor to conceptualize various non-monetary resources. Academics such as Becker (1975), Bourdieu (1986) and Coleman (1988) were central in popularizing the use of the terms 'human capital', 'cultural capital' and 'social capital', and these terms were quickly adopted by academics and researchers. They are now commonplace in both policy documents and the mainstream media, as well as in the academic literature.

Whilst attractive because of their purported ability to explain social and economic inequality, these concepts all share a fatal flaw; they are extremely difficult to operationalize. Part of the problem stems from the definition of the concepts themselves. The original proponents of these constructs do not provide sufficiently precise directions about what resources do and do not count as any of the various forms of 'capital', much less do they outline how each form of capital should be operationalized and measured. Sullivan (2002) observes that Bourdieu, for example, does not clearly define 'cultural capital' and as a consequence the concept has been operationalized in many different ways. This makes comparing research that uses the concept practically impossible, as most studies have defined the concept differently and used different indicators in order to measure it. While these studies use the same terminology, most are actually measuring something that is subtly different to all the others. This does not necessarily weaken individual pieces of research or invalidate their findings, as long as they are transparent about their definitions and indicators, but it does render the concept of 'cultural capital' of little use because its meaning is not transferable between studies. The sheer variety of different ways it has been used by researchers dramatically reduces its usefulness and demonstrates the lack of consensus surrounding its meaning. In fact, using a concept that has no shared meaning can present problems for the synthesis of research findings and facilitate, if not encourage, misinterpretation of research findings.

Blackburn (2003) notes that one of the fundamental problems with these non-economic 'capitals' is that they often appear to cover a seemingly vast range of resources. This lack of precision not only allows large inconsistencies between studies in terms of their definition and operationalization but also means that the very 'breadth of coverage…removes any explanatory potential' (Blackburn 2003, p. 6). Much of the research that has relied on various forms of 'capital' to explain their findings have brought us no closer to understanding the various phenomena they set out to explain. Indeed, some researchers appear to use the terms as a substitute for formulating their own explanations for their research findings (see White 2007).

Blackburn (2003) also objects to the use of the term 'capital' on more fundamental grounds. He argues that referring to human, social or cultural resources as forms of 'capital' is both inaccurate and misleading. The use of the term implies both that there is some kind of parallel with the properties of economic capital and that 'social capital', for example, is something more than mere social resources. He demonstrates that these so-called 'forms of capital' share very few similarities with economic capital and display many characteristics that are completely incompatible with it. Whilst economic capital is reduced by expenditure, for example, 'social capital' appears unaffected or even increased by its use. These alternative 'forms of capital' are not coherent or useful even at the level of metaphor, let alone as theoretical constructs. He ends by stating that while 'there is nothing, other than common sense and clarity, to stop anything being labelled "capital"' (p. 6), 'in view of the traditional meaning, this extended application is inappropriate, misleading and generally unhelpful' (p. 9).

Another frequently used concept is Bourdieu's notion of 'habitus'. Despite the notoriously difficult language used by Bourdieu and problems of translation even acknowledged by his English translator (Nice 1997) his concepts are very popular amongst some researchers as explanations of social (especially *class*) reproduction. However, in a rare critical evaluation of Bourdieu's use of the term, Sullivan's (2002, p. 144) careful analysis reveals that 'the concept of habitus is theoretically incoherent and has no clear use for empirical researchers'. In relation to some recent educational research, she concludes that this concept adds little, the main use of the concept being to add a 'veneer of sophistication to empirical findings' (Sullivan 2002, p. 150).

Whilst it may be fashionable to bring particular theoretical concepts into the research process, either in initial research questions or in attempts to answer those questions, doing so does not necessarily make research any easier or more valuable. In fact, as is illustrated in the examples above, it can raise a number of inter-related problems with no guarantee of any reward for this effort. The usefulness of many commonly cited theoretical concepts is questionable, and they are often adopted as explanations in an entirely uncritical manner. It is best for novice researchers to avoid the use of these concepts in research questions, unless they are crucial to the test of a particular hypothesis. Even when this is a specific aim of a study it is likely that, because of their vague definition or unclear relationship to a wider theory, many of them will be untestable in any real sense. And, as was explained in Chapter 1, ideas that are not amenable to testing cannot be characterized as 'theory' in any meaningful sense of the term.

Key Points

- Even commonly used social scientific concepts can be difficult to define and operationalize
- Only use concepts that are essential to your research – don't be tempted to 'follow fashion'

SUMMARY

This chapter started by arguing for question-led, rather than methods-led, research. The importance of thinking about questions first, and being unduly influenced by preferences for particular methods was outlined alongside a discussion of the important differences between research *methods* and research *design*. It was argued that research design was a central element of all research, regardless of the questions addressed or the methods of data collection and analysis used.

The problems that can occur when attempting to operationalize the key concepts used in your study were also discussed. This has hopefully alerted you to the importance of thinking about definitions and indicators early on in the research process and also highlighted some of the ways in which any difficulties can be resolved.

The next and final chapter in this book examines the way in which social researchers answer research questions. The discussion focuses on the ways in which the answers are presented and justified, rather than on the answers themselves. This is an issue that is directly related to research design, as the logic underlying the design of a study is central in 'warranting' any conclusions that are drawn.

FURTHER READING

There are hundreds of research methods texts currently on the market. I would, however, particularly recommend the following for their originality, clarity or just plain usefulness:

Booth, W.C., Columb, G.G. & Willlams, J.M. (2003) *The Craft of Research*. (2nd Edn.) Chicago, IL: University of Chicago Press.
Denscombe, M. (2002) *Ground Rules for Good Research: A 10 Point Guide for Social Research*. Buckingham: Open University Press.
Gorard, S. (2003a) *Quantitative Methods in Social Science*. London: Continuum.
Gorard, S. with Taylor, C. (2004) *Combining Methods in Educational and Social Research*. Maidenhead: Open University Press.
Punch, K.F. (1998) *Introduction to Social Research: Quantitative and Qualitative Approaches*. London: Sage.
Robson, C. (1993) *Real World Research: A Resource for Social Scientists and Practitioner-Researchers*. Oxford: Blackwell.

Bryman's text is also recommended for its comprehensive coverage:

Bryman, A. (2004) *Social Research Methods*. 2nd Edn. Oxford: Oxford University Press.

de Vaus's text is, in my opinion, the best text available on research design:

de Vaus, D.A. (2001) *Research Design in Social Research*. London: Sage.

5 Answering research questions: claims, evidence and warrant

If there is one topic that is even more neglected than the formulation of research questions, it is the issue of how such questions should be answered. Or, more specifically, how answers to research questions can be presented in a way that allows readers to evaluate a researcher's claims.

Many methods texts cover issues relating to the presentation of *data* but very few discuss the relationship between that data (or 'evidence') and the conclusions that are drawn. This omission is significant, as making and supporting claims about what a particular study has demonstrated is not a simple matter. In fact, it can actually be one of the most difficult challenges faced by a researcher (Booth et al. 2003).

Establishing a coherent argument, based on a transparent and valid chain of reasoning between the available evidence and the conclusions drawn, is a vital part of the research process. This is because it allows readers to judge whether the claims you make (i.e. the answers to your research questions) are adequately supported by the evidence you present. As such, this element of the research process is as important as any other but one that is not always given sufficient attention, even by professional researchers (Gorard 2002b).

In this chapter several issues relating to the process of linking evidence and conclusions are explored, including the nature of claims, data and evidence; the role of qualifiers; and the importance of alternative hypotheses. The most important topic addressed, however, is the idea of 'warrant'. This term will probably be unfamiliar to most readers, at least in this context, and of all the concepts in this chapter it is perhaps the most difficult to grasp. Readers who wish to explore this topic further are advised to refer to Booth et al. (2003), Toulmin (1964) and Toulmin et al. (1979).

THE STRUCTURE OF ARGUMENTS

The structure of arguments has been studied in great depth by philosophers, logicians, and linguists but has received much less attention amongst social scientists. While many issues in this area continue to be the subject of considerable debate, a degree of consensus has emerged regarding the relationship between evidence and claims. Most commentators share the belief that three features are of central importance (Gorard 2002b). A claim must always be supported by an evidence base. This evidence, however, must be linked to the claim via a 'warrant' in order to demonstrate its relevance to that claim. Arguments, therefore, should proceed as follows:

claim → *warrant* → *evidence*

This chain of reasoning is essential if arguments are to be subjected to rational assessment (Toulmin 1964). But whilst it is common for researchers to present two of these elements – a claim and an evidence base – it is rarely the case that they are explicit about the warrant that links the data to their conclusions (Gorard 2002b). Indeed, warrants are often noticeable only by their absence (Booth et al. 2003). However, as is argued in the remainder of this chapter, they are as important as both the claims that are made and the evidence that is provided to support those claims.

Commentators in the area of argumentation often use different terminology to describe identical, or similar, elements of an argument. Commonly used terms include data, evidence, reason, claim, conclusion, warrant and backing. Some of these terms are, arguably, interchangeable (such as data and evidence, claim and conclusion) whilst others refer to elements of an argument's structure that are not covered in this chapter. As the aim here is to introduce readers to the general principles of warranting claims, debates surrounding the use of particular terms are side-stepped. A simplified model is presented and, for the most part, only the terms 'evidence', 'warrant' and 'claim' are used.

> **Key Points**
>
> - Your conclusions should always be linked to the evidence you present via a 'warrant'
> - A warrant is a logical argument demonstrating why your conclusions follow from your evidence

CLAIMS

Toulmin et al. (1979, p. 29) define claims as 'assertions put forward for general acceptance'. Answering a research question generally involves making a claim of some kind (Booth et al. 2003), even if the answer is an admission of ignorance or of the inconclusiveness of the evidence available. Researchers are expected not only to make claims, however, but to defend them (Booth et al. 2003). Because of this, it is necessary not only to be cautious about the kinds of claims that are made (Denscombe 2003) but to ensure that the links between your claims and the available evidence have been carefully thought through.

The kind of conclusions that can be drawn from a particular study will depend upon both the kind of research questions you have formulated (Booth et al. 2003) and the nature of the available data. As discussed in Chapter 4, the type of data generated in an investigation will be linked to the research questions via a research design. By the time you have worked through the processes of formulating research questions and constructing an appropriate research design, it should be very clear what kind of claims you will be able to make. For example, cross-sectional data may allow historical trends to be established but longitudinal data are necessary if conclusions are to be drawn about how individuals change over time. Similarly, claims about cause and effect are unlikely to be justified outside of some type of experimental research design. It is important to be aware of the limitations of your chosen design and not to go beyond your evidence base when making claims about what your research has demonstrated.

Like research questions, claims should not be vague – as this leads to vague arguments – and should be stated clearly and precisely.

What is considered to be appropriate precision, however, tends to vary between disciplines and fields of study (Booth et al. 2003), and claims that appear to be unrealistically precise are unlikely to be viewed as credible by readers or reviewers (Bordage 2001). Booth et al. (2003, p. 147) suggest that, for example, 'a historian would seem foolhardy if she asserted that the Soviet Union reached its point of collapse at 2 p.m. on August 18, 1987'. As is the case when formulating research questions, the degree of precision required will vary from case to case and decisions in this area can only be made using your judgement rather than by referring to a set of rules or guidelines.

Qualifying claims

As all studies have limitations it is important that you recognize these, outline them explicitly in your research report (Bordage 2001) and consider the consequences for any claims that you make (Denscombe 2002). Being appropriately cautious about the extent to which the research findings can be generalized is vital and you should also provide an indication as to how conclusive you believe the evidence to be (Marshall & Rossman 1999, Gorard 2002b). As Booth et al. (2003, p. 135) argue, 'no claim is free from limiting conditions ... [and]only rarely can you assert in good conscience that you are 100 percent certain that your evidence is 100 percent reliable and your claims are unqualifiedly true'. Claims are generally more credible when their limitations have been clearly set out.

Qualifying claims can be a difficult balancing act as 'every claim is subject to countless conditions' but specifying too many caveats can be viewed as 'fudging' the issue (Booth et al. 2003, p. 135). Avoiding terms such as 'always', 'every', 'never', and so on is usually advisable when making general claims, however. Such language may be appropriate when describing your *data* but, as most findings in social science are probabilistic rather than deterministic (i.e. they describe or explain things that are *usually* but not *always* the case) such terms are only very rarely appropriate when drawing conclusions. While coming from a high income background may increase and individual's chance of entering higher education, for example, it does not always guarantee it. Even if all the data in a study suggested the former conclusion, only one counter-example would be needed to disprove this, so it would be unwise to make such a claim.

The extent to which claims are subjected to scrutiny by the research community will often depend on the degree to which they are viewed as significant or controversial. Warrants tend to be stated more frequently, and in greater detail, when the authors anticipate that their claims will be challenged (Booth et al. 2003) and, as argued below, you should always consider plausible alternative explanations for your data. Several commentators (e.g. Gorard 2002b, Shavelson et al. 2003) insist that making warrants explicit should be standard practice in research reports, regardless of how the conclusions are expected to be received. Indeed, this might be the simplest way of improving the quality of social research, as it would focus the minds of both researchers and readers on the type of claims that can logically follow from a particular evidence base.

Key Points

- Any claims you make or conclusions that you reach should be stated clearly and precisely
- It is wise to err on the side of caution when making claims. Make sure you 'qualify' your claims appropriately
- You should be prepared to defend your claims against alternative interpretations of your data

---

DATA AND EVIDENCE

Writers on argumentation invariably refer to 'data' or 'evidence'. Some use one term and not the other, while others use them interchangeably. Booth et al. (2003, p. 39) distinguish the two, arguing that 'data are inert...until you use them as *evidence* to support a *claim*' (Booth et al. 2003). Whilst acknowledging that the distinction is not necessarily a simple one, debates on terminology are not strictly relevant to the issues raised in this chapter and both terms are treated as interchangeable in the following discussions, as are the terms 'claim' and 'conclusion'. Gorard (2002b), for example, characterizes the structure of an argument using the following terms:

data → *warrant* → *conclusion*

This model reverses the direction of the reasoning in the previous example and uses slightly different terminology. Nevertheless, the key principle – of linking claims/conclusions to evidence/data via a warrant – remains the same.

Differentiating between evidence, claims and warrant

The most important point to make about evidence is that it is different from both claims and warrant. Gorard (2002b) reports that when one group of academics, working on a high status multi-million pound research programme, were asked to specify their warrant they often described either their methods of data collection and/or analysis, research design, conclusions (claims) or the nature of their data. Only a small minority actually described the links between their data and conclusions, demonstrating that, at least in one field of social research, even those leading the field are not clear about the meaning of the term. A warrant is necessary regardless of the research methods used in a study, although the logic of some research designs (e.g. experiments) imply a warrant that is relatively straightforward (Gorard 2002b). It is important that warrants are not confused with either evidence or claims, as each of these elements occupies a different place in the structure of an argument.

WARRANT

'Warrants are the most abstract, difficult element in an argument to understand and manage' (Booth et al. 2003, p. 165). As already noted, they are rarely stated explicitly in research reports but are essential if arguments are to be evaluated rationally (Toulmin 1964). Gorard (2002b, p. 136) defines a warrant as simply a 'logical and persuasive link between the evidence produced and the conclusions drawn'.

A warrant should aim to convince a reader that the evidence presented is relevant to the claim being made and to outline the chain of reasoning that links the two. It should seek to demonstrate that a particular claim is the most likely explanation for the evidence that has been collected and, in doing so, show why plausible alternative explanations are less likely (see below).

Warrants work by appealing to widely accepted principles of reasoning that work at a more general level than the particular argument being constructed. These principles, of which there are many, must be ones that are 'so deeply embedded in our assumptions and tacit knowledge that we would never question them' (Booth et al. 2003, p. 168). One of the problems with stating warrants, however, is that we often rely on these assumptions to support our arguments *implicitly*, simply because they are so taken for granted. Since they form the bedrock of much of our thinking, we rarely make them explicit, for to do so seems either unnecessary, or patronizing to our audience. In fact we sometimes may not even consciously recognize that we are using these basic principles of reasoning.

However, it is sometimes necessary, when warranting claims, to explicitly reference these assumptions or principles, in order to show the reasoning that underlies the link between a particular claim and a particular piece of evidence. This alerts the reader to 'the *general ways of arguing* being applied in [a] particular case and *implicitly relied on* as ones whose *trustworthiness* is well established' (Toulmin et al. 1979, p. 43). The aim is to show that the reasoning being relied upon to link a particular body of evidence to specific claim is well established and widely accepted.

A very simple example of an accepted principle of reasoning, that could be relied upon as a warrant is the following:

> *Principle A*
> *If a greater number of a particular phenomena are observed at one point of time than had been observed at a previous point in time, this constitutes evidence of a 'rise' or 'increase' in the frequency of this phenomenon.*

This principle can be applied to a hypothetical set of data relating to the number of crimes committed in a particular region, presented in Table 5.1 below.

Table 5.1 An example of evidence and a claim

Evidence		Claim
Crimes at Time 1	Crimes at Time 2	Crime has increased
100	150	

Table 5.2 Using a warrant to link evidence and a claim

Evidence		Warrant	Claim
Crimes at Time 1	Crimes at Time 2	Principle A (see above)	Crime has increased
100	150		

The claim in Table 5.1 may appear to be self-evident given the evidence that is provided. Indeed, in such a case it is often easy to confuse the *evidence* with the *claim* itself. The connection between any particular claim and any body of evidence, however, *always* relies on a chain of reasoning connecting the two. This chain of reasoning is the warrant. The link between the evidence and the claim in Table 5.1 actually relies on the acceptance of Principle A, described above. Table 5.2 includes this warrant, showing the principle of reasoning that links the evidence to the claim.

When writing up a research project, the exact nature of such a claim would need to be clarified in greater detail, and also tempered by appropriate qualifying terms (see previous discussion, above). It would be necessary to know, for example, whether there had been any changes in the size of the target population over the period studied. If the population had grown, it might be expected that the number of crimes would also rise proportionally, leading to an increase in the *frequency* of criminal activity but not necessarily any increase in the crime *rate* (which is a proportional measure). Other contextual factors, such as changes in the law or methods of recording crime would also have to be examined before the claim could be properly formulated.

Whatever the final form of the claim, however, the principle of reasoning being appealed to support it is unlikely to be questioned, as it is generally acknowledged as sound. Its applicability in this *particular situation* – that is its validity as a warrant – may be questioned, however, and other principles may be put forward as more relevant. Following from a point raised in the previous paragraph, it may be suggested that increases in the frequency of any phenomenon (in this case crime) must be measured in relation to changes in the size of a reference group (in this case the population of interest). The relevance of this principle could be decided by reference to the exact nature of the claim (was it concerned with absolute or relative changes?) and the nature of the evidence (did the region's population grow over the period studied?). However, owing to their widespread use and acceptance, the soundness of the principle of reasoning *itself* (i.e. Principle A) would generally be taken as read, and individuals who challenged such principles would be unlikely to be taken seriously.

While the example above may seem trivial, Gorard (2002) cites research published in a peer-reviewed academic journal that appears to ignore this principle. Waslander and Thrupp (1995) actually present data that show *decreasing* levels of the socio-economic status (SES) of students as evidence of the *increasing* SES of that group and, even after being challenged, still claim that this conclusion is justified. While this is an extreme example of violating a very basic, and universally accepted, principle of reasoning, countless examples of more subtle misinterpretations are common (see Paulos 1996, Brignell 2000, Best 2001, 2003).

Warrants for research claims in social science are unlikely to be as simple as the above example. They are often explanatory, rather than descriptive, and may relate to more than one source of evidence. They can be part of a hierarchy within which the strength of a warrant for one claim depends on the acceptance of another claim, which must also be warranted. All warrants, however, must at some point be grounded in a principle of reasoning that is more or less universally accepted.

Booth et al. (2003) suggest that these general principles can be of various types, such as cause and effect (X always leads to Y), one-thing-is-the-sign-of-another (X signals Y), a rule of behaviour (X's always do Y), a definition (X's always possess quality Y) and so on. However, all general principles of reasoning, and therefore warrants, share the following form (Booth et al. 2003, p. 168):

When (ever) X, then Y

It is this kind of reasoning that should ultimately underpin any warrant and link a claim to a body of evidence.

Key Points

- It is important to differentiate between your evidence, your conclusions and the argument that links the two ('warrant').
- Warrants should provide 'a logical and persuasive link' between the evidence being presented and the claims being made.
- Warrants should ultimately rest on principles of reasoning that are universally accepted.
- Warrants should be made explicit in <u>all</u> research reports, regardless of the methods used in a study.

ALTERNATIVE HYPOTHESES

As already noted, one of the most important reasons to present a warrant is to make a case for the particular claim being proposed being more plausible than the infinite number of other explanations for ending up with a particular set of data. In addition to demonstrating the plausibility of one particular explanation, a well-constructed warrant will also be effective in ruling out alternative accounts (Shavelson et al. 2003). The consideration of 'rival hypotheses' (Huck & Sandler 1979) is central to the construction of a strong warrant and a strategy that is a central element in any investigation (de Vaus 2001).

Before presenting your case to an audience, either verbally or in writing, you must first convince yourself that your favoured explanation is the most likely of all the plausible alternatives (Medawar 1979). This is particularly important if you had a strong hunch about what the research might reveal or believed that a particular theory would be either supported or undermined by your findings. As was discussed in Chapter 1, the capacity to be surprised is an essential prerequisite for the conduct of research of any kind.

It is best not to wait until alternative explanations are suggested by critics (or examiners) of your work and it is good practice to get into the habit of *actively* generating plausible alternative explanations for your findings (Bordage 2001, de Vaus 2001). You can then evaluate the credibility of these alternative explanations by comparing the strength of the warrant required to connect each claim to the evidence base produced in your study. This will not only increase you confidence in the conclusions you have drawn but will also prepare you to defend them against any criticisms.

SUMMARY

Providing answers to research questions is one of the most challenging aspects of the research process. Far from being a simple matter of presenting the findings of a study, it involves making claims, and using a warrant to link these claims to the evidence. This process is often neglected when research reports are published and close examination of the claims made by many authors reveal that insufficient attention has been paid to making logical connections between the available data and the conclusions that are drawn. Considering plausible alternative explanations for the existence of a particular evidence base is a useful test of the strength of a warrant and good researchers should be in the habit of always questioning their claims. As Kerlinger (1986, p. 23) notes, 'it is the business of scientists to doubt most explanations of phenomena'. This should include their own.

FURTHER READING

Both Booth et al. and Toulmin et al. provide accessible introductions to warranting claims, while Gorard presents a case for their importance:

Booth, W.C., Columb, G.G. & Williams, J.M. (2003) *The Craft of Research.* (2nd Edn.) Chicago, IL: University of Chicago Press.

Gorard, S. (2002) 'Fostering Scepticism: The Importance of Warranting Claims', *Evaluation and Research in Education*, 16 (3), pp. 136–49.

Toulmin, S., Rieke, R. & Janik, A. (1979) *An Introduction to Reasoning.* New York: Macmillan. ch. 3.

Afterword

Formulating research questions is the first step in the research process and providing answers to these questions is the last. This book has aimed to demonstrate that the questions that we ask are connected, intimately and inextricably, to nearly every stage of research. Meaningful, productive, useful research *must* be driven by a genuine curiosity, and researchers should be prepared to be surprised by what they discover.

Investigations should always be led by questions, not by methods or ideological or political agendas. Researchers must be willing to learn new skills in order to answer the questions that concern them, and should not restrict themselves to addressing particular types of questions just because they can be answered using methods that they are comfortable using.

More care needs to be taken in both formulating and answering research questions. Research questions need to be discussed more frequently and in greater depth, and should feature in many more methods texts than is currently the case. They are an essential part of the research process that is, at present, largely neglected.

Conclusions, though often confused with findings, are different, and are never self-evident. More attention needs to be paid to how we answer the questions we ask. The idea of 'warranting' is central to this challenge, and we should all aim to be transparent about the logical link of reasoning between the claims we make and the evidence we present.

This text represents an attempt to remedy the lack of attention paid to research questions in much of the current literature. I hope that it is followed by many more contributions in this area, and is helpful to those who read it.

Bibliography

Abrahamson, M. (1983) *Social Research Methods.* Englewood Cliffs, NJ: Prentice-Hall.

Ainley, P. & Bailey, B. (1997) *The Business of Learning: Staff and Student Experiences of Further Education in the 1990s.* London: Cassell.

Andrews, R. (2003) *Research Questions.* London: Continuum.

Ball, S.J., Maguire, M. & Macrae, S. (2000) *Choice, Pathways and Transitions Post-16: New Youth, New Economies in the Global City.* London: RoutledgeFalmer.

Bechhofer, F. & Patterson, L. (2000) *Principles of Research Design in the Social Sciences.* London: Routledge.

Becker, G. (1975) *Human Capital.* New York: National Bureau of Economic Research.

Bell, J. (1993) *Doing Your Research Project: A Guide for First Timers in Education and Social Science.* 2nd Edn. Milton Keynes: Open University Press.

Berg, B.L. (2004) *Qualitative Research Methods for the Social Sciences.* 5th Edn. Boston, MA: Pearson.

Best, J. (2001) *Damned Lies and Statistics: Untangling Numbers from the Media, Politicians, and Activists.* London: University of California Press.

Best, J. (2003) *More Damned Lies and Statistics: How Numbers Confuse Public Issues.* London: University of California Press.

Black, T.R. (1993) *Evaluating Social Science Research: An Introduction.* London: Sage.

Blackburn, R. (2003) 'The Concept of Capital: Sense and Nonsense', paper presented to SSRG Conference, Cardiff 2003.

Blastand, M. & Dilnot, A. (2007) *The Tiger That Isn't: Seeing through a World of Numbers.* London: Profile.

Booth, W.C., Columb, G.G. & Williams, J.M. (2003) *The Craft of Research.* 2nd Edn. Chicago, IL: University of Chicago Press.

Bordage, G. (2001) 'Reasons Reviewers Reject and Accept Manuscripts: The Strengths and Weaknesses in Medical Education Reports', *Academic Medicine,* 76 (9), pp. 889–96.

Bourdieu, P. (1986) 'The Forms of Capital', in Richardson, J.G. (Ed.) *Handbook of Theory and Research for the Sociology of Education.* New York: Greenwood Press.

Bradley, D.B. (2001) 'Developing Research Questions through Grant Proposal Development', *Educational Gerontology*, 27, pp. 569–81.

Brignell, J. (2000) *Sorry, Wrong Number! The Abuse of Measurement*. London: Brignell Associates/European Science & Environment Forum.

Bryman, A. (1988) *Quantity and Quality in Social Research*. London: Unwin Hyman.

Bryman, A. (2004) *Social Research Methods*. 2nd Edn. Oxford: Oxford University Press.

Bulmer, M. (1979) 'Block 2A: Beginning Research', *Open University Module DE304 Research Methods in Education and the Social Sciences*. Milton Keynes: Open University Press. ISBN 0 355 07436 7.

Campbell, J.P., Daft, R.L. & Hulin, C.L. (1982) *What to Study: Generating and Developing Research Questions*. Beverley Hills, CA: Sage.

Coakley, J. & Dunning, E. (Eds) (2002) *Handbook of Sports Studies*. London: Sage.

Coe, R. & Fitz-Gibbon, C. (1998) 'School Effectiveness Research: Criticisms and Recommendations', *Oxford Review of Education*, 24 (4), pp. 421–38.

Coleman, J.S. (1988) 'Social Capital in the Creation of Human Capital', *American Journal of Sociology*, 94, pp. 95–120.

Collins, H.M. (1985) *Changing Order: Replication and Induction in Scientific Practice*. London: Sage.

Collins, M.F. with Kay, T. (2002) *Sport and Social Inclusion*. London: Routledge.

Cozby, P.C., Worden, P.E. & Kee, D.W. (1989) *Research Methods in Human Development*. Mountain View, CA: Mayfield.

Creswell, J.W. (2003) *Research Design: Qualitative, Quantitative and Mixed Methods Approaches*. 2nd Edn. Thousand Oaks, CA: Sage.

Crompton, R. (1998) *Class and Stratification: An Introduction to Current Debates*. 2nd Edn. Cambridge: Polity.

de Vaus, D.A. (2001) *Research Design in Social Research*. London: Sage.

Denscombe, M. (2002) *Ground Rules for Good Research: A 10 Point Guide for Social Research*. Buckingham: Open University Press.

Dillon, J.T. (1983) 'The Use of Questions in Educational Research', *Educational Researcher*, 12 (9), pp. 19–24.

Dillon, J.T. (1984) 'The Classification of Research Questions', *Review of Educational Research*, 54 (3), pp. 327–61.

Dillon, J.T. (1988) 'The Remedial Status of Student Questioning', *Journal of Curriculum Studies*, 20 (3), pp. 197–210.

Dobbert, M.L. (1982) *Ethnographic Research: Theory and Application for Modern Schools and Societies*. New York: Praeger.

Dunning, E., Murphy, P., Waddington, I. & Astinakis, A.E. (Eds) (2002) *Fighting Fans: Football Hooliganism as a World Phenomenon*. Dublin: University of Dublin Press.

ESRC (2007) 'About ESRC' http://www.esrcsocietytoday.ac.uk/ESRCInfo Centre/about/ (accessed on 18 August 2008)

Farrington, D.P. (2004) *Gender Differences in Risk Factors for Offending*. London: Home Office.

Ferns, W. & Riedel, M. (1995) 'The Expert System as a Metaphor', in Hess, P. & Mullen, E. (Eds) *Practitioner-Researcher Partnerships: Building Knowledge from in and for Practice*. London: NASW Press.

Fischer, D.H. (1970) *Historians' Fallacies: Toward a Logic of Historical Thought*. New York: Harper & Row.

Fisher, M. (2002) 'The Role of Service Users in Problem Formulation and Technical Aspects of Social Research', *Social Work Education*, 21 (3), pp. 305–12.

Fitz-Gibbon, C. (2000) 'Education: Realising the Potential', in Davies, H., Nutley, S. & Smith, P. (Eds) *What Works? Evidence-Based Policy and Practice in Public Services*. Bristol: Policy Press.

Fitz-Gibbon, C. (2001) *Value Added for Those in Despair: Research Methods Matter*. London: British Psychological Society.

Flick, U. (1998) *An Introduction to Qualitative Research*. London: Sage.

Gigerenzer, G. (2003) *Reckoning with Risk: Learning to Live with Uncertainty*. 2nd Edn. London: Penguin.

Glaser, B.G. & Strauss, A.L. (1967) *The Discovery of Grounded Theory: Strategies for Qualitative Research*. Mill Valley, CA: Sociology Press.

Goldstein, H. (2003) *Multilevel Statistical Models*. 3rd Edn. London: Arnold.

Gorard, S. (2002a) 'Can We Overcome the Methodological Schism? Four Methods for Combining Qualitative and Quantitative Evidence', *Research Papers in Education*, 17 (4), pp. 345–61.

Gorard, S. (2002b) 'Fostering Scepticism: The Importance of Warranting Claims', *Evaluation and Research in Education*, 16 (3), pp. 136–49.

Gorard, S. (2003a) *Quantitative Methods in Social Science*. London: Continuum.

Gorard, S. (2003b) 'What Is Multi-Level Modelling for?', *British Journal of Education Studies*, 51 (1), pp. 46–63.

Gorard, S. (2003c) 'Comments on "Modelling Social Segregation" by Goldstein, H. & Noden, P.', *Oxford Review of Education*, 30 (3), pp. 435–40.

Gorard, S. (2007) 'The Dubious Benefits of Multi-Level Modeling', *International Journal of Research and Method in Education*, 30 (2), pp. 221–36.

Gorard, S. & Rees, G. (1999) 'Two Dimensions of Time: The Changing Social Context of Lifelong Learning', *Studies in the Education of Adults*, 31 (1), pp. 35–48.

Gorard, S. & Rees, G. (2002) *Creating a Learning Society? Learning Careers and Policies for Lifelong Learning*. Bristol: Policy Press.

Gorard, S., See, B.H., Smith, E. & White, P. (2006a) *Teacher Supply: The Key Issues*. London: Continuum.

Graziano, A.M. & Raulin, M.L. (2004) *Research Methods: A Process of Inquiry*. 5th Edn. Boston, MA: Pearson.

Greer, S. (1969) 'On the Selection of Problems', Ch. 1, *The Logic of Social Inquiry*. Chicago, IL: Aldine. (reprinted in Bynner, J. & Stribley, K.M. (Eds) (1979) *Social Research: Principles and Procedures*. London: Longman: Open University Press).

Greer, S. (1978) 'On the selection of problems', in J. Bynner & K.M. Stribley (eds) *Social Research: principles and procedures*. Harlow, Essex: Longman/Open University Press.

Guba, E.G. & Lincoln, Y.S. (1994) 'Competing Paradigms in Qualitative Research', in Denzin, N.K. & Lincoln, Y.S. (Eds) *Handbook of Qualitative Research*. 1st Edn. pp. 105–17. Thousand Oaks, CA: Sage.

Hakim, C. (2000) *Research Design: Successful Designs for Social and Economic Research*. 2nd Edn. London: Routledge.

Halfpenny, P. (1982) *Positivism and Sociology: Explaining Social Life*. London: Allen & Unwin.

Hamblin, C.L. (1967) 'Questions', in Edwards, P. (Ed.) *The Encyclopedia of Philosophy: Volume 7*. New York: Macmillan & The Free Press. pp. 49–53.

Hammersley, M. (1999) *Taking Sides in Social Research: Essays on Partisanship and Bias in Social Enquiry*. London: Routledge.

Hammersley, M. & Atkinson, P. (1995) *Ethnography: Principles in Practice*. 2nd Edn. London: Routledge.

Heimer, K. (2006) *Gender and Crime: Patterns of Victimization and Offending*. New York: New York University Press.

Holliday, A. (2002) *Doing and Writing Qualitative Research*. London: Sage.

Home Office (1997) *Aspects of Crime: Gender*. London: Home Office.

Huck, S.W. & Sandler, H.M. (1979) *Rival Hypotheses: Alternative Interpretations of Data Based Conclusions*. New York: Harper & Row.

Hudson-Barr, D. (2005) 'From Research Idea to Research Question: The Who, What, Where, When and Why', *Journal for Specialists in Paediatric Nursing*, 10 (2), pp. 90–2.

Huff, D. (1973) *How to Lie with Statistics*. London: Penguin.

Janesik, V.J. (2000) 'The Choreography or Qualitative Research Design', in Denzin, N.K. & Lincoln, Y.S. (Eds) *Handbook of Qualitative Research*. 2nd Edn. pp. 379–99. Thousand Oaks, CA: Sage.

Jarvie, G. (2006) *Sport, Culture and Society: An Introduction*. London: Routledge.

Jevons, W.S. (1958: 1874) *The Principles of Science : A Treatise on Logic and Scientific Method*. London: Macmillan.

Jorgenson, D.L. (1989) *Participant Observation: A Methodology for Human Studies*. Applied Social Research Methods Series Volume 15. Newbury Park, CA: Sage.

Kane, E. (1984) *Doing Your Own Research: Basic Descriptive Research in the Social Sciences and Humanities*. London: Marion Boyars.

Kerlinger, F.N. (1973) *Foundations of Behavioural Research*. 2nd Edn. New York: CBS Publishing.

Kerlinger, F.N. (1986) *Foundations of Behavioural Research*. 3rd Edn. New York: CBS Publishing.

Labovitz, S. & Hagedorn, R. (1971) *Introduction to Social Research*. New York: McGraw-Hill.

Lewins, F. (1992) *Social Science Methodology: A Brief but Critical Introduction*. South Melbourne: Macmillan.

Lewis, I. & Munn, P. (1997) *So You Want to Do Research! A Guide for Beginners on How to Formulate Research Questions*. Edinburgh: Scottish Council for Research in Education.

Locke, L.F., Silverman, S.J. & Spirduso, W.W. (2004) *Reading and Understanding Research*. 2nd Edn. Thousand Oaks, CA: Sage.

Lundstedt, S. (1968) 'A Note on Asking Questions', *Journal of General Psychology*, 79, pp. 229–39.

Macintyre, C. (2000) *The Art of Action Research in the Classroom*. London: David Fulton.

Marshall, C. & Rossman, G.B. (1999) *Designing Qualitative Research*. 3rd Edn. Thousand Oaks, CA: Sage.

Mason, J. (1996) *Qualitative Researching*. London: Sage.

Medawar, P.B. (1972) *The Hope of Progress*. London: Methuen.

Medawar, P.B. (1979) *Advice to a Young Scientist*. New York: Harper & Row.

Miles, J. & Shevlin, M. (2001) *Applying Regression and Correlation: A guide for Students and Researchers*. London: Sage.

Miles, M.B. & Huberman, A.M. (1994) *Qualitative Data Analysis: An Expanded Sourcebook*. Thousand Oaks, CA: Sage.

Milton, P. (2000) 'Mind the Gap! Translating Practice Problems into Research Questions in an Evaluation of a Welfare Programme', *European Journal of Social Work*, 3 (1), pp. 25–8.

Mitchell, R. (2001) 'Multilevel Modelling Might Not Be the Answer', *Environment and Planning A*, 33, 1357–60.

Morash, M. (2006) *Understanding Gender, Crime and Justice*. London: Sage.

Morrison, J. (2002) 'Developing Research Questions in Medical Education: The Science and the Art', *Medical Education*, 36, pp. 596–7.

Mullen, E.J. (2002) 'Problem Formulation in Practitioner Partnerships: A Decade of Experience at the Center for the Study of Social Work Practice', *Social Work Education*, 21 (3), pp. 323–36.

Nachmias, D. & Nachmias, C. (1976) *Research Methods in the Social Sciences*. London: Edward Arnold.

Nice, R. (1997) 'Bourdieu and Bernstein', Plenary Lecture, *Pierre Bourdieu: Language, Culture and Education. An International Conference.* Southampton University, UK, 17–18 April, 1997.

Paulos, J.A. (1996) *A Mathematician Reads the Newspaper.* London: Penguin,

Paulos, J.A. (2001) *Innumeracy: Mathematical Illiteracy and Its Consequences.* 2nd Edn. New York: Hill and Wang.

Platt, J. (1976) *Realities of Social Research; An Empirical Study of British Sociologists.* New York: Wiley.

Pole, C.J. & Lampard, R. (2002) *Practical Social Investigation: Qualitative and Quantitative Methods in Social Research.* Harlow: Prentice Hall.

Popper, K. (1959; 2002) *The Logic of Scientific Discovery.* London: Routledge.

Popper, K. (1972) *Conjectures and Refutations: the Growth of Scientific Knowledge.* 4th Edn. London: Routledge & Kegan Paul.

Prandy, K. (2002) 'Measuring Quantities: The Qualitative Foundation of Quantity', *Building Research Capacity,* 2, April 2002, pp. 3–4. ISSN 1475–4193.

Punch, K.F. (1998) *Introduction to Social Research: Quantitative and Qualitative Approaches.* London: Sage.

Reason, P. (1994) 'Three Approaches to Participative Enquiry', in Denzin, N.K. & Lincoln, Y.S. (Eds) *Handbook of Qualitative Research.* 1st Edn. Thousand Oaks, CA: Sage.

Robson, C. (1993) *Real World Research: A Resource for Social Scientists and Practitioner-Researchers.* Oxford: Blackwell.

Rose, D. & Pevalin, D.J. (Eds) (2003) *A Researchers Guide to the National Statisitics Socio-Economic Classification.* London: Sage.

Sarantakos, S. (1998) *Social Research.* 2nd Edn. Basingstoke: Palgrave.

Scriven, M. (1998) 'Minimalist Theory: The Least Theory That Practice Requires', *The American Journal of Evaluation,* 19 (1), 57–72.

Sellitz, C., Jahoda, M., Deutch, M. & Cook, S.W. (1965) *Research Methods in Social Relations.* London: Methuen.

Selwyn, N. & Robson, K. (1998) 'Using Electronic Mail as a Research Tool', Social Research Update, 21, pp. 1–4.

Shavelson, R., Phillips, D., Towne, L. & Feuer, M. (2003) 'On the Science of Education Design Studies', *Educational Researcher,* 32 (1), pp. 25–8.

Shaw, M.E. & Costanzo, P.R. (1970) *Theories of social psychology.* New York: McGraw-Hill, 1970.

Shulman, L.S. (1988) 'Disciplines of Inquiry in Education: An Overview', in Jaeger, R.M. (Ed.) *Complementary Methods for Research in Education.* Washington, DC: AERA.

Smith, E. (2005) *Analysing Underachievement in Schools.* London: Continuum.

Smith, E. (2008) *Using Secondary Data in Educational and Social Research*. Maidenhead: Open University Press.

Smith, T.L. & Mathae, K.B. (2004) 'National Science Foundation Budget in the FY 2005 Budget', in *AAAS Report XXIX: Research and Development in FY 2005*. New York: AAAS.

Soydan, H. (2002) 'Formulating Research Problems in Practitioner-Researcher Partnerships', *Social Work Education*, 21 (3), pp. 287–304.

Spradley, J.P. (1980) *Participant Observation*. New York: Holt, Rinehart & Winston.

Stone, P. (2002) 'Deciding upon and Refining a Research Question', *Palliative Medicine*, 16, pp. 265–7.

Sullivan, A. (2002) 'Bourdieu and Education: How Useful Is Bourdieu's Theory for Researchers?', *Netherlands' Journal of Social Sciences*, 38 (2), pp. 144–66.

Tashakkori, A. & Teddlie, C. (1998) *Mixed Methodology: Combining Qualitative and Quantitative Approaches*. Thousand Oaks, CA: Sage.

Taylor, C. (2002) 'The RCBN Consultation Exercise: Stakeholder Report', *Cardiff University School of Social Sciences Occasional Paper 50*. Cardiff: Cardiff University.

Toulmin, S.E. (1964) *The Uses of Argument*. Cambridge: Cambridge University Press.

Toulmin, S., Rieke, R. & Janik, A. (1979) *An Introduction to Reasoning*. New York: Macmillan.

Tymms, P. & Taylor Fitz-Gibbon, C. (2002) 'Theories, Hypotheses, Hunches and Ignorance', *Research Capacity Building*, 2, April 2002, pp. 10–11. ISSN 1475–4193.

Verma, G.K. & Beard, R.M. (1981) *What Is Educational Research? Perspectives on Techniques of Research*. Aldershot: Ashgate.

Walklate, S. (2004) *Gender, Crime and Criminal Justice*. 2nd Edn. London: Willan.

Waslander, S. & Thrupp, M. (1995) 'Choice, Competition, and Segregation: An Empirical Analysis of a New Zealand School Market, 1990–93', *Journal of Education Policy*, 10 (1), pp. 1–26.

White, P. (2007) *Education and Career Choice: A New Model of Decision Making*. London: Palgrave.

White, P., Gorard, S., Fitz J. & Taylor, C. (2001) 'Regional and Local Differences in Admission Arrangements', *Oxford Review of Education*, 27 (3), pp. 317–37.

Williams, B. (1989) 'The Idea of Equality', in Cosin, B., Flude, M. & Hales, M. (Eds) *School, Work and Equality*. London: Hodder & Stoughton.

Yin, R.K. (1989) *Case Study Research*. Thousand Oaks, CA: Sage.

Yun, G.W. & Trumbo, C.W. (2000) 'Comparative Response to a Survey Executed by Post, Email and Web-Form', *Journal of Computer-Mediated Communication*, 6, www.ascusc.org/jcmc/vol6/yun.html (accessed 2 September 2008)

Index

abstraction, 23, 68, 100, 106
advice, expert, 11, 20
aims and objectives, 33–5, 52
analysis, 104
   quantitative, 101
   qualitative
articles, journal, 11–12, 29

capital, economic, cultural and social,
   107–9
claims, **114–16**
   and evidence, 113
   qualifying, **115–16**
   unwarranted, 76, 120
comparison, **51–2**, **75–6**, 88, 103–4
   of research findings, 108
   of secondary data, 104
   of warrants, 122
computer aided qualitative data analysis
   software (CAQDAS), 95
concepts, 25–6, 67–8, *see also* definition
   unoperational, **106–10**
curiosity, 123
   and methods, 96
   and surprise, 5–7

data, 37–9
   collection, 98–9
   collection questions (DCQs), **45–6**,
      105
   cross-sectional and longitudinal, 114
   and evidence, **116–17**
   historical, 74–5
   population, 72–3
   secondary, 85, 104
   and social class, 103–4
   and sub-questions, 64
   unnecessary, 35, 62
   and warrant, 116–17
databases, bibliographic, 8
definition, 67–9, 99–102
   of concepts, 34–5, 41

of terms, 43–5
documents, policy, 27–9

*Economic and Social Research Council
   (ESRC)*, 75, 78
'empirical criterion', 90
empowerment, **50–1**
epistemology, 91–3
   interpretivist and positivist, 91–2
evidence, 35, 42–3, 98–101, **112–22**
   and data, **116–17**
explanations, 51–2, 108–9
   alternative, 116, 121–2
   existing, 13
   incomplete, 17
   and theory, 23–4

geographic coverage, **73–4**

historical
   context, **74–5**
   trends, 114
hypotheses, 5–6, 36, **53–7**
   alternative, 54, **121–2**
   and ethnographic research, 56–7
   and intuition, 56
   null, 54
   and 'qualitative' research, 56–7
   and research design, 56–7
   testing of, 54, 109–10
   and theory, 24–5

influence, **21–2**, *see also* originality
   of beliefs and preferences, 5
   of existing thought, 7, 13

jargon, *see* language
journals, academic, 8, 11–13, 29

language, 34, **66–77**, 115
   academic, 68–9
   and brevity, **66–7**

clarity of, **67–9**
and jargon, 69, 87
and precision, **69–72**
technical, 68
literature
gaps in the, 17–19
policy, 28–9
review of, 11–16
theoretical, 25–6

measurement, 100–8, 119–20
'methodolatry', **93–7**
methods
-led research, **93–7**
mono-, 92, 94–6
'qualitative', 25, 56–7, 97–8
'quantitative', 25, 53, 56–7, 97
'multi-level modelling' (MLM), 94, 126

newspapers, 9
broadsheet, 9, 28
tabloid, 28

ontology, 92
operationalization, 100–10
originality, 16, **18–21**, *see also* influence
and 'new' data, 19–20

population of interest, 71–2, **72–3**, 104,
119–20
problems
of content, **42–6**
of form, 35–41
practitioner and practice, 13–14,
29–31
research, 56, 94, 97
social, 9–10, 27–9

questions
contributory and ancillary, 63–5
data collection, **45–6**
descriptive and explanatory, 39, **47–52**
main and subsidiary, **63–5**
metaphysical, 42–3
and methods, 89–91

normative, **43–5**
number of, **64–5**
popular, 21, 62
prioritizing of, **61–2**
researchable and unresearchable, 30,
59–66, 84
scope of, **60–84**, 87, 94
tautological, **40–1**
types of, **47–52**
'W-questions', 42–3, **48–9**
'why' questions, 42, 48

replication, 17–20
research, *see also* methods
aims, **33–5**, 105–6
applied, 10, 13–15, **29–31**
objectives, **33–5**
policy, 10, **27–9**, 50–1, 75, 83
topics, 15, **33–5**, 70, 92
research design, 19–22, 56–7, 77–82,
85–8, 89–96, **97–9**, 110
importance of, **97–9**
and 'qualitative' research, 97–8, 101
resources, 61–2, **78–88**
financial, **78–84**
human, 85–6

social class, 40–1, **102–6**
Statistical Package for Social Scientists
(SPSS), 81, 95

texts
handbooks, 9, 13
introductory, 12–13
recommended, 9
theory
and data, 24
explanatory, 23–4, 108
generation, **24–6**
grounded, 13
testing and verification, **24–6**

variables, dependent and independent, 54

warrant, **117–22**